INFANT/TODDLER ENVIRONMENT RATING SCALE

REVISED EDITION

Updated with additional notes and a new expanded scoresheet

THELMA HARMS **DEBBY CRYER** **RICHARD M. CLIFFORD**

Frank Porter Graham Child Development Institute
The University of North Carolina at Chapel Hill

TEACHERS COLLEGE PRESS

TEACHERS COLLEGE | COLUMBIA UNIVERSITY

NEW YORK AND LONDON

Published by Teachers College Press, 1234 Amsterdam Avenue, New York, NY 10027

Cover design by Peter Paul Connolly

ISBN-13: 978-0-8077-4640-0
ISBN-10: 0-8077-4640-1

Printed on acid-free paper

Manufactured in the United States of America

20   19   18   17   11   10   9   8   7

Contents

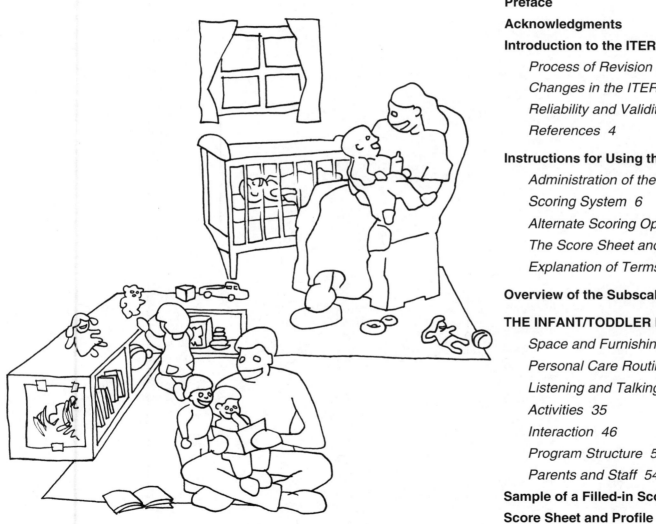

Preface to the Updated Edition

This updated edition of the ITERS-R is not a revision. It contains all of the ITERS-Revised Edition with all items and indicators intact. It also includes several helpful additions such as:

- The widely used Additional Notes available on our website
- A new Expanded Scoresheet, which incorporates a number of reminders and tables to assist in scoring the items
- An improved spiral binding

This updated edition was produced in response to requests from many scale users who faithfully pasted the Additional Notes into their scales because they found them helpful in establishing and maintaining their accuracy using the ITERS-R. The new Expanded Scoresheet, which we have used so far in various states in our own training sessions, has also proved very helpful to both experienced and novice assessors. We hope that these additions to the ITERS-R make the scale easier to use.

We are grateful to Lisa Waller for her help in developing the Expanded Scoresheet, to Tracy Link for providing assistance with the new additional notes, and to Elisa Allen, who so ably incorporated the additional materials into this updated edition. As always, feedback from our staff of expert assessors, Cathy Riley, Lisa Waller, Kris Lee, Tracy Link, and Elisa Allen, as well as many other users of the scale, has been extremely helpful.

For additional explanations of the meaning of ITERS-R requirements see *All About the ITERS-R* (2004), D. Cryer, T. Harms, C. Riley. Lewisville, NC: Pact House Publishing, ISBN-10: 0-88076-615-8.

Acknowledgments

Over the years, our work has been enriched by the many colleagues in the United States, Canada, Europe, and Asia, who have used the Infant/Toddler Environment Rating Scale in research, program improvement, and monitoring, and have generously shared their insights with us. This open, collegial discussion with scale users has prompted us to think more profoundly, and has been extremely beneficial. We want especially to thank the many people who responded to our questionnaire with ideas for the ITERS revision. We read and considered every suggestion, and although it is not possible to thank each one of you personally, we want you to know how meaningful your guidance was as we considered revisions.

We want to recognize in particular:

- The participants in the focus group on inclusion and diversity issues held in Chapel Hill: Wanda Ferguson, Adele Ray, Theresa Sull, Marti Brown, Marie Gianino, Tanya Clausen, Anne Carver, Amy Hoglund, Quwanya Smith, Beth Jaharias, Sarah Hurwitz, Valerie Wallace, Stephanie Ridley, Betty De Pina, Vicki Cole, Melissa Miller, and Giselle Crawford.
- The observers who collected the field test data and, at the end of the field test, gave us their valuable critique: Cathy Riley, Lisa Waller, Kris Fulkerson, Megan Porter, Kim Winton, and Lisa Ann Gonzon.
- Megan Porter who so ably organized and directed the field test.

- Special thanks to Cathy Riley, Lisa Waller, Kris Fulkerson, and Megan Porter for detailed feedback and valuable suggestions.
- Ethan Feinsilver, assisted by Mary Baldwin, for their attention to detail in preparing the manuscript.
- Susan Liddicoat, our editor at Teachers College Press, for her patience and determination.
- David Gardner for his careful analysis of the field test data.
- Research and child care center staff of the Frank Porter Graham Child Development Institute, for their continuing support of our work.
- Child care center staff in the local Raleigh–Durham–Chapel Hill community, for playing a very important role in our work by allowing us to conduct observations in their classrooms.
- Dr. Don Bailey, Director of the Frank Porter Graham Child Development Institute, for awarding a small grant to support the ITERS Revision Focus Group.
- The A.L. Mailman Family Foundation, Luba Lynch, Executive Director, and Betty Bardige, Chair, for funding the field test and the video training package, and especially for their faith in us and in the value of our work.

Thelma Harms, Debby Cryer, and Richard M. Clifford
Frank Porter Graham Child Development Institute
August, 2002

Introduction to the ITERS–R

The Infant/Toddler Environment Rating Scale–Revised Edition (ITERS–R) is a thorough revision of the original Infant/Toddler Environment Rating Scale (ITERS, 1990). It is one of a series of four scales that share the same format and scoring system but vary considerably in requirements, because each scale assesses a different age group and/or type of child development setting. The ITERS–R retains the original broad definition of environment including organization of space, interaction, activities, schedule, and provisions for parents and staff. The 39 items are organized into seven subscales: Space and Furnishings, Personal Care Routines, Listening and Talking, Activities, Interaction, Program Structure, and Parents and Staff. This scale is designed to assess programs for children from birth to 30 months of age, the age group that is most vulnerable physically, mentally, and emotionally. Therefore, the ITERS–R contains items to assess provision in the environment for the protection of children's health and safety, appropriate stimulation through language and activities, and warm, supportive interaction.

Admittedly, it is very challenging to meet the needs of infants and toddlers in a group care setting because each of these very young children requires a great deal of personal attention in order to thrive. The economic pressure of raising a family continues to make the use of out-of-home group care for infants and toddlers the norm rather than the exception. Therefore, as a society, we are increasingly aware that we must face the challenge of providing child care settings for very young children that promote optimal development. It has long been the personal challenge of professional early childhood educators to provide the nurturance and stimulation that very young children need on a daily basis. A comprehensive, reliable, and valid instrument that assesses process quality and quantifies what is observed to be happening in a classroom, can play an important role in improving the quality of infant/toddler care.

In order to define and measure quality, the ITERS–R draws from three main sources: research evidence from a number of relevant fields (health, development, and education), professional views of best practice, and the practical constraints of real life in a child care setting. The requirements of the ITERS–R are based on what these sources judge to be important conditions for positive outcomes in children both while they are in the program and long afterward. The guiding principle here, as in all of our environment rating scales, has been to focus on what we know to be good for children.

Process of Revision

The process of revision drew on four main sources of information: (1) research on development in the early years and findings related to the impact of child care environments on children's health and development; (2) a content comparison of the original ITERS with other assessment instruments designed for a similar age group, and additional documents describing aspects of program quality; (3) feedback from ITERS users, solicited through a questionnaire that was circulated and also put on our website, as well as from a focus group of professionals familiar with the ITERS; and (4) intensive use for more than two years by two of the ITERS co-authors and over 25 ITERS trained assessors for The North Carolina Rated License Project.

The data from studies of program quality gave us information about the range of scores on various items, the relative difficulty of items, and their validity. The content comparison helped us to identify items to consider for addition or deletion. By far the most helpful guidance for the revision was the feedback from direct use in the field. Colleagues from the US, Canada, and Europe who had used the ITERS in research, monitoring, and program improvement gave us valuable suggestions based on their experience with the scale. The focus group discussed in particular what was needed to make the revised ITERS more sensitive to issues of inclusion and diversity.

Changes in the ITERS–R

While retaining the basic similarities in format and content that provide continuity between the ITERS and ITERS–R, the following changes were made:
1. The indicators under each level of quality in an item were numbered so that they could be given a score of "Yes", "No", or "Not Applicable" (NA) on the scoresheet. This makes it possible to be more exact in reflecting observed strengths and weaknesses in an item.
2. Negative indicators on the minimal level were removed from one item and are now found only in the 1 (inadequate) level. In levels 3 (minimal), 5 (good), and 7 (excellent) only indicators of positive attributes are listed. This eliminates the one exception to the scoring rule in the original ITERS.
3. The Notes for Clarification have been expanded to give additional information to improve accuracy in scoring and to explain the intent of specific items and indicators.

4. Indicators and examples were added throughout the scale to make the items more inclusive and culturally sensitive. This follows the advice given to us by scales users to include indicators and examples in the scale instead of adding a subscale.
5. New items were added to several subscales including the following:
   - Listening and Talking: Item 12. Helping children understand language, and Item 13. Helping children use language.
   - Activities: Item 22. Nature/science, and Item 23. Use of TV, video and/or computer.
   - Program Structure: Item 30. Free play, and Item 31. Group play activities.
   - Parents and Staff: Item 37. Staff continuity, and Item 38. Supervision and evaluation of staff.
6. Some items in the Space and Furnishings subscale were combined to remove redundancies, and two items were dropped in Personal Care Routines: Item 12. Health policy, and Item 14. Safety policy. Research showed that these items were routinely rated with high scores because they were based on regulation but the corresponding items assessing practice were rated much lower. It is practice that the ITERS–R should concentrate on since the aim is to assess process quality.
7. The scaling of some of the items in the subscale Personal Care Routines was made more gradual to better reflect varying levels of health practices in real life situations, including Item 6. Greeting/departing, Item 7. Meals/snacks, Item 9. Diapering/toileting, Item 10. Health practices, and Item 11. Safety practices.
8. Each item is printed on a separate page, followed by the Notes for Clarification.
9. Sample questions are included for indicators that are difficult to observe.

Reliability and Validity

As noted earlier in this introduction, the ITERS–R is a revision of the widely used and documented ITERS, that is one in a family of instruments designed to assess the overall quality of early childhood programs. Together with the original instrument, the Early Childhood Environment Rating Scale (ECERS), and the more recent revision of that scale, the ECERS–R, these scales have been used in major research projects in the United States as well as in a number of other countries. This extensive research has documented both the ability of the scales to be used reliably and the validity of the scales in terms of their relation to other measures of quality and their tie to child development outcomes for children in classrooms with varying environmental ratings.

In particular, both the ECERS and ITERS scores are predicted by structural measures of quality such as child-staff ratios, group size and staff education levels (Cryer, Tietze, Burchinal, Leal, & Palacios, 1999; Phillipsen, Burchinal, Howes, & Cryer, 1998). The scores are also related to other characteristics normally expected to be related to quality such as teacher salaries and total program costs (Cryer et al., 1999; Marshall, Creps, Burstein, Glantz, Robeson, & Barnett, 2001; Phillipsen et al., 1998; Whitebook, Howes, & Phillips, 1989). In turn, rating scale scores have been shown to predict children's development (Burchinal, Roberts, Nabors, & Bryant, 1996; Peisner-Feinberg et al., 1999).

Since the concurrent and predictive validity of the original ITERS is well established and the current revision maintains the basic properties of the original instrument, the studies of the ITERS–R have focused on the degree to which the revised version maintains the ability of trained observers to use the scale reliably. Additional studies will be needed to document the continued relationship with other measures of quality as well as to document its ability to predict child outcomes. A two-phase study was completed in 2001 and 2002 to establish reliability in use of the scale.

The first phase was a pilot phase. In this phase a total of 10 trained observers in groups of two or three used the first version of the revised scale in 12 observations in nine centers with infant and/or toddler groups. After these observations, modifications were made in the revised scale to adjust for issues that arose in the pilot observations.

The final phase of the field test involved a more formal study of reliability. In this phase, six trained observers conducted 45 paired observations. Each observation lasted approximately three hours, followed by a 20–30 minute teacher interview. The groups observed were selected to be representative of the range of quality in programs in North Carolina. North Carolina has a rated license system that awards points for various features related to quality. Centers are given a license with one to five stars depending on the total number of points earned. A center receiving a one-star license meets only the very basic requirements in the licensing law while a five-star center meets much higher standards. For our sample we selected 15 groups in centers with one or two stars, 15 with three stars, and 15 with four or five stars. The programs were also chosen to represent various age ranges of children served. Of the 45 groups observed, 15 were from groups with children under 12 months of age, 15 from groups with children 12–24 months old, and 15 with children 18–30 months old. The groups were in 34 different centers and seven of them included children with identified disabilities. All centers were in the central portion of North Carolina.

The field test resulted in 90 observations with two paired observations each in 45 group settings. Several measures of reliability have been calculated.

Indicator Reliability. Across all 39 items in the revised ITERS, there are a total of 467 indicators. There was agreement on 91.65% of all indicator scores given by the raters. Some researchers will omit the Parents and Staff Subscale in their work. Thus, we have calculated the indicator reliability for the child specific items in the first six subscales, Items 1–32. The observer agreement for the 378 indicators in these items was 90.27%. Only one item had indicator agreement of less than 80% (Item 11. Safety practices was 79.11%). The item with the highest level of indicator agreement was Item 35. Staff professional needs, with an agreement of 97.36%. It is apparent that a high level of observer agreement at the indicator level can be obtained using the ITERS–R.

Item Reliability. Because of the nature of the scoring system, it is theoretically possible to have high indicator agreement but low agreement at the item level. Two measures of item agreement have been calculated. First, we calculated the agreement between pairs of observers within 1 point on the seven-point scale. Across the 32 child-related items, there was agreement at this level 83% of the time. For the full 39 items, agreement within 1 point was obtained in 85% of the cases. Item agreement within one point ranged from a low of 64% for Item 4. Room arrangement, to 98% for Item 38. Evaluation of staff.

A second, somewhat more conservative measure of reliability is Cohen's Kappa. This measure takes into account the difference between scores. The mean weighted Kappa for the first 32 items was .55 and for the full 39-item scale it was .58. Weighted Kappa's ranged from a low of .14 for Item 9. Diapering/toileting, to a high of .92 for Item 34. Provisions for personal needs of staff. Only two items had weighted Kappa's below .40 (Item 9. Diapering/ toileting, and Item 11. Safety practices, with a weighted Kappa of .20). In both cases the mean item score was extremely low. A characteristic of the Kappa statistic is that for items with little variability the reliability is particularly sensitive to even minor differences between observers. The authors and observers agreed that the low scores on these items accurately reflected the situation in the groups observed and that any changes to substantially increase variability would provide an inaccurate picture of the features of quality reflected in these two items. For all items with a weighted Kappa below .50 the authors examined the items carefully and made minor changes to improve the reliability of the item without changing its basic content. These changes are included in the printed version of the scale. Even using the more conservative measure of reliability, the overall results indicate a clearly acceptable level of reliability.

Overall Agreement. For the full scale, the intraclass correlation was .92 both for the full 39 items as well as for the 32 child-related items. Intraclass correlations for the seven subscales are shown in Table 1. It should be noted that the intraclass correlation for the Program Structure Subscale is calculated excluding Item 32. Provision for children with disabilities, since only a small portion of groups received a score on this item. Taken together with the high levels of agreement at the item level, the scale has clearly acceptable levels of reliability. It should be remembered that this field test used observers who had been trained and had a good grasp of the concepts used in the scale.

Table 1 Intraclass Correlations of Subscales

Subscale	Correlation
Space and Furnishings	0.73
Personal Care Routines	0.67
Listening and Talking	0.77
Activities	0.91
Interaction	0.78
Program Structure	0.87
Parents and Staff	0.92
Full Scale (Items 1–39)	0.92
All Child Items (1–32)	0.92

Internal Consistency. Finally we examined the scale for internal consistency. This is a measure of the degree to which the full scale and the subscales appear to be measuring a common concept. Overall the scale has a high level of internal consistency with a Cronbach's alpha of .93. For the child-related items, 1–32, the alpha is .92. This measure indicates a high degree of confidence that a unified concept is being measured. A second issue is the degree to which the subscales also show consistency. Table 2 shows the alphas for each subscale:

Table 2 Internal Consistency

Subscale	Alpha
Space and Furnishings	0.47
Personal Care Routines	0.56
Listening and Talking	0.79
Activities	0.79
Interaction	0.80
Program Structure	0.70
Parents and Staff	0.68
Full Scale (Items 1–39)	0.93
All Child Items (1–32)	0.92

Cronbach's alphas of .6 and higher are generally considered acceptable levels of internal consistency. Thus, caution should be taken in using the Space and Furnishings and Personal Care Routines subscales. Program Structure, Item 32. Provisions for children with disabilities was rated for only the few groups that had children with identified disabilities. The internal consistency score for this subscale was calculated excluding this item. Thus, the authors recommend using the Program Structure subscale excluding Item 32 unless most programs being assessed include children with disabilities.

Overall, the field test demonstrated a high level of interrater agreement across the scale items and at the full-scale score level. These findings are quite comparable to those found in similar studies of the original ITERS and ECERS, and the ECERS-R. All of these previous studies have been confirmed by the work of other researchers, and the scales have proven to be quite useful in a wide range of studies involving the quality of environments for young children. At the same time the scales have been shown to be user-friendly to the extent that it is possible to get observers to acceptable levels of reliability with a reasonable level of training and supervision.

References

American Academy of Pediatrics, American Public Health Association, and National Resource Center for Health and Safety in Child Care. (2002). *Caring for Our Children: The National Health and Safety Performance Standards for Out-of-Home Child Care, 2nd edition.* Elk Grove Village, IL: American Academy of Pediatrics.

Burchinal, M., Roberts, J., Nabors, L., & Bryant, D. (1996). Quality of center child care and infant cognitive and language development. *Child Development, 67,* 606–620.

Cryer, D., Tietze, W., Burchinal, M., Leal, T., & Palacios, J. (1999). Predicting process quality from structural quality in preschool programs: A cross-country comparison. *Early Childhood Research Quarterly, 14*(3).

Marshall, N. L., Creps, C. L., Burstein, N. R., Glantz, F. B., Robeson, W. W., & Barnett, S. (2001). *The Cost and Quality of Full Day, Year-round Early Care and Education in Massachusetts: Preschool Classrooms.* Wellesley, MA: Wellesley Centers for Women and Abt Associates, Inc.

Phillipsen, L., Burchinal, M., Howes, C., & Cryer, D. (1998). The prediction of process quality from structural features of child care. *Early Childhood Research Quarterly, 12,* 281–303.

Peisner-Feinberg, E. S., Burchinal, M. R., Clifford, R. M., Culkin, M. L., Howes, C., Kagan, S. L., Yazejian, N., Byler, P., Rustici, J., & Zelazo, J. (1999). *The children of the cost, quality, and outcomes study go to school: Technical report.* Chapel Hill: University of North Carolina at Chapel Hill, Frank Porter Graham Child Development Center.

Whitebook, M., Howes, C., & Phillips, D. (1989). *Who cares? Child care teachers and the quality of care in America. National child care staffing study.* Oakland, CA: Child Care Employee Project.

Instructions for Using the ITERS–R

It is important to be accurate in using the ITERS–R whether you use the scale in your own classroom for self-assessment or as an outside observer for program monitoring, program evaluation, program improvement, or research. A video training package for the ITERS–R is available from Teachers College Press for use in self-instruction or as part of group training. It is preferable to participate in a training sequence led by an experienced ITERS–R trainer before using the scale formally. The training sequence for observers who will use the scale for monitoring, evaluation, or research should include at least two practice classroom observations with a small group of observers led by an experienced group leader, followed by an interrater agreement comparison. Additional field practice observations may be needed to reach the desired level of agreement, or to develop reliability within a group. Anyone who plans to use the scale should read the following instructions carefully before attempting to rate a program.

Administration of the Scale

1. The scale is designed to be used with one room or one group at a time, for children from birth through 30 months of age. A block of at least three hours should be set aside for observation and rating if you are an outside observer, that is, anyone who is not a member of the teaching staff (i.e., program directors, consultants, licensing personnel, and researchers).

2. Before you begin your observation, complete the identifying information on the top of the first page of the Score Sheet. You will need to ask the teacher for some of the information, especially the birth dates of the oldest and youngest children, number of children enrolled in the group, and whether there are children with identified disabilities in the group. By the end of the observation, make sure all identifying information requested on the first page is complete.

3. Take a few minutes at the beginning of your observation to orient yourself to the classroom.
   - You may want to start with Items 1–5 in Space and Furnishings because some of the indicators are easy to observe and typically do not change during the observation.
   - Some items require observation of events and activities that occur only at specific times of the day (i.e., Items 6–9 in Personal Care Routines, Item 16. Active physical play). Be aware of those items so that you can observe and rate them as they occur.

- Score items that assess aspects of relationships only after you have observed for a sufficient time to get a representative picture (i.e. Items 13–14 on language, Items 25–28 on interactions).
- Item 14. Using books and Items 15–24 in the Activities subscale will require both inspection of materials and observation of use of materials.

4. Be careful not to disrupt the ongoing activities while you are observing.
   - Maintain a pleasant but neutral facial expression.
   - Do not interact with the children unless you see something dangerous that must be handled immediately.
   - Do not talk to or interrupt the staff.
   - Be careful about where you place yourself in the room to avoid disrupting the environment.

5. Arrange a time with the teacher to ask questions about indicators you were not able to observe. The teacher should be free of responsibility for children when he or she is answering questions. Approximately 20–30 minutes will be required for questions. In order to make best use of the time set aside for asking questions:
   - Use the sample questions provided, whenever applicable.
   - If you have to ask questions about items for which no sample questions have been provided, note your questions on the score sheet or another sheet of paper before talking with the teacher.
   - Ask only those questions needed to decide whether a higher score is possible.
   - Ask questions on one item at a time following the order of the items in the scale and take notes or decide on a score before you move on to the next item.

6. Note that the ten-page Score Sheet, starting on page 63, provides a convenient way to record the ratings for indicators, items, subscale, and total scores, as well as your comments. The Profile that follows the Score Sheet permits a graphic representation of this information.
   - A fresh copy of the Score Sheet is needed for each observation. Permission is hereby given to photocopy the Score Sheet and Profile only, not the entire scale.
   - Ratings should be recorded on the Score Sheet before leaving the program or immediately afterward. Ratings should not be entrusted to memory for later recording.

- Complete an assessment, including any report that is required, before doing another observation.
- It is advisable to use a pencil with a good eraser on the Score Sheet during the observation, so that changes can be made easily.

Scoring System

1. Read the entire scale carefully, including the Items, Notes for Clarification, and Questions. In order to be accurate, all ratings must be based as exactly as possible on the indicators provided in the scale items.
2. The scale should be kept readily available and read constantly during the entire observation to make sure that the scores are assigned accurately.
3. Examples that differ from those given in the indicator but meet the intent of the indicator may be used as a basis for giving credit for an indicator.
4. Scores should be based on the current situation that is observed or reported by staff, not on future plans. In the absence of observable information on which to base your rating, you may use answers given by the staff during the question period to assign scores.
5. Requirements in the scale apply to *all* children in the group being observed, unless an exception is noted in an item.
6. When scoring an item, always start reading from 1 (inadequate) and progress upward till the correct quality score is reached.
7. Yes (Y) is marked on the scoresheet if the indicator is *true* for the situation being observed. No (N) is marked on the scoresheet if the indicator is *not true*. (For each numbered indicator, ask yourself, "Is this true, Yes or No?").
8. Ratings are to be assigned in the following way:
   - A rating of 1 must be given if *any* indicator under 1 is scored Yes.
   - A rating of 2 is given when all indicators under 1 are scored No and at least half of the indicators under 3 are scored Yes.
   - A rating of 3 is given when all indicators under 1 are scored No and all indicators under 3 are scored Yes.
   - A rating of 4 is given when all requirements of 3 are met and at least half of the indicators under 5 are scored Yes.
   - A rating of 5 is given when all requirements of 3 are met and all indicators under 5 are scored Yes.
   - A rating of 6 is given when all requirements of 5 are met and at least half of the indicators under 7 are scored Yes.
   - A rating of 7 is given when all requirements of 5 are met and all indicators under 7 are scored Yes.

- A score of NA (not applicable) may only be given for indicators or for entire items when "NA permitted" is shown on the scale and there is an NA on the Score Sheet. Indicators that are scored NA are not counted when determining the rating for an item, and items scored NA are not counted when calculating subscale and total scale scores.
- To calculate average subscale scores, sum the scores for each item in the subscale and divide by the number of items scored. The total mean scale score is the sum of all item scores for the entire scale divided by the number of items scored.

Alternate Scoring Option

Since each one of the indicators in the ITERS–R can be given a rating, it is possible to continue to rate the indicators beyond the quality level score assigned to an item. Using the scoring system described above, indicators are typically rated only until an item quality score is assigned. However, if it is desirable, for purposes of research or program improvement, to gain additional information on areas of strength beyond the item quality level score, the observer can continue to rate all the indicators in an item.

If the alternate scoring option is selected and all indicators are scored, the required observation time and the questioning time will need to be extended considerably. An observation of approximately three and a half to four hours and a questioning time of approximately 45 minutes will be required to complete all indicators. The additional information may, however, be helpful in making plans for specific improvements and in the interpretation of research findings.

The Score Sheet and the Profile

The Score Sheet provides for both indicator and item scores. The indicator scores are Y (Yes), N (No), and NA (not applicable), which is permitted only as noted for selected indicators. The item quality scores are 1 (Inadequate) through 7 (Excellent), and NA (not applicable), which is permitted only as noted for selected items. There is also a small space provided for notes to justify the scores. Since notes are particularly helpful in counseling staff for improvement, we suggest taking more extensive notes on another sheet of paper for this purpose.

Care should be taken to mark the correct box under Y, N, or NA for each indicator. The numerical item quality score should be circled clearly (see sample, p. 62).

Item 12. While indicators for quality in this item hold true across a diversity of cultures and individuals, the ways in which they are expressed may differ. For example, tone of voice may differ, with some individuals using excited voices while others may be quieter. Whatever the personal communication styles of the staff members being observed, the requirements of the indicators must be met, although there can be some variation in the way that this is done. Because the frequency of language interactions is very important in influencing the development of children's language abilities, score indicators based on what is observed as a regular practice throughout the observation. Examples of meeting the requirements should occur throughout the observation, not just as single instances.

1.2. Noise from an adjacent room should also be considered if it is disruptive.

1.3. Score "Yes" if an unpleasant tone is used or negative things are said three or more times during the observation, even if many positive verbal interactions are also observed.

3.1. Staff must talk to the children during both care routines and play to give credit.

3.3. No more than two examples of staff using a mildly negative tone can be observed to give credit. Do not give credit if staff ever use an extremely unpleasant or harsh tone with the children.

3.4. The content of staff talk must be encouraging and positive about 75% of the time, and neutral the rest of the time.

5.1. Although there can be variation in the amount of talking done by different staff members, *all* staff must use a neutral or pleasant tone. Staff talk must be either pleasant or neutral, and no long periods of silence on the part of staff should be observed.

5.4. In determining whether the language is descriptive, ask yourself if you could tell what staff are talking about to children just by listening and not looking.

Inadequate		Minimal		Good		Excellent
1	2	3	4	5	6	7

13. Helping children use language*

1.1 Little or no positive response to children's attempts to communicate through gestures, sounds, or words.*

1.2 Staff often ignore or respond negatively to children's attempts to communicate.

3.1 Moderate amount of verbal or non-verbal positive response to children's attempts to communicate throughout the day; little or no ignoring of children or negative response.*

3.2 Some attempts to correctly interpret what the child is trying to communicate throughout the day (Ex. staff try another way to calm crying child if first solution does not work; try hard to understand toddler's unclear words).*

5.1 Staff generally respond in a timely and positive manner to children's attempts to communicate (Ex. crying is answered quickly; children's verbal requests are attended to; respond with interest to children's communications during play).*

5.2 Staff add words to the actions they take in responding to children throughout the day (Ex. "I'm changing your diaper. Now you are all dry! Doesn't that feel better?").*

5.3 Staff are skillful at interpreting children's attempts to communicate and frequently follow through appropriately (Ex. "I know you're hungry; let's go get a snack." "Are you tired of playing with those blocks? Here are the books. No? Oh, you want me to hold you.").*

7.1 Staff have many turn-taking conversations with children (Ex. imitate infant sounds in a back-and-forth "baby conversation"; repeat what toddler says and then let toddler take another turn at talking).

7.2 Staff add more words and ideas to what children say (Ex. when child says "juice" staff respond with "Here is your orange juice. It's in your cup.").*
NA permitted.

7.3 Staff ask children simple questions (Ex. ask baby a question and then give answer: "What's in this picture? It's a dog with a bone."; wait for toddlers to answer before giving an answer).*

7.4 Staff usually maintain a good balance between listening and talking (Ex. give child time to process information and answer; talk more for babies and give toddlers more time to talk themselves).

(See Notes for Clarification on next page)

Item 13. When determining percentage of staff response to children, it is not necessary to calculate an exact percentage. Instead, base score on the prevalent practice.

1.1. Score "Yes" if staff tend to respond positively to children's attempts to communicate significantly less than half of the time.

3.1. "Moderate amount" requires a positive response by staff at least half of the time children attempt to communicate, no negative responses to children, and little or no ignoring of children's attempts to communicate.

3.2. At least half the time throughout the observation, staff must be observed attempting to correctly interpret what children try to communicate.

5.1. To give credit, staff immediately give a positive response to children's attempts to communicate at least 75% of the time, and there should be no negative responses or lengthy waits for children who are obviously in need. Observe to assure that staff are paying close attention and responding to all children in the group, including those who are not as demanding as others.

5.2. Many examples should be observed during both care routines and play in order to give credit.

5.3. To give credit, staff must succeed in correctly interpreting what children mean at least 75% of the time and successfully act to meet the children's needs with few exceptions.

7.2. NA permitted when no verbal children are present.

7.3. At least two instances of staff asking simple questions, waiting for an answer, and answering for children if they cannot answer by themselves must be observed to give credit.

14. Using books

1.1 Fewer than 6 appropriate infant/toddler books accessible daily for much of the day.*	3.1 At least 6 appropriate infant/toddler books (but no less than 1 for each child in the group) accessible daily, for much of the day.*	5.1 At least 12 appropriate infant/toddler books (but no less than 2 for each child in the group) accessible daily for much of the day.*	7.1 Book area set up for toddlers to use independently.* *NA permitted*
1.2 Books generally in poor repair (Ex. torn or incomplete books; tattered pictures; books scribbled on).*	3.2 Almost all books are in good repair.*	5.2 A wide selection of books is accessible.*	7.2 Staff are involved in using books with children periodically throughout the day.*
1.3 Staff do not use books with children.*	3.3 Staff are involved in using books with children daily (either staff- or child-initiated).*	5.3 Staff read books daily with individuals or very small groups of interested children.*	7.3 Books are added or changed to maintain interest.*
	3.4 Participation encouraged only while children are interested; children not forced to participate.	5.4 Book times are warm and interactive (Ex. infant held while book is read; toddler allowed to turn pages and point to pictures).*	

Notes for Clarification

1.1, 3.1, 5.1. Examples of appropriate books: sturdy vinyl, cloth, or hard-page books with pictures suitable for infants and toddlers. Books may be home-made or commercially produced. Books for older children or adults do not count to meet the requirements of this item.

1.2. Score "Yes" if more than 50% of the accessible books are in poor repair.

1.3. Score "Yes" if staff are not observed using books with children and if staff report that books are used less than three times a week with children.

3.1. Count only complete books with covers and all pages to give credit for the indicator. Books that are not appropriate for the children in the group (e.g., too difficult, too easy, frightening, violent) cannot be counted as any of the 6 required books.

3.1, 5.1. The number of books required is based on the maximum daily attendance permitted in the classroom, not on the number of children present on any particular day.

3.2. Good repair means that the book has an intact cover and the pages are not torn, scribbled on, or missing. Minor problems (small tears, slight scribble, chew marks) that do not interfere with the use of the books are acceptable. For almost all books to be in good repair requires that no more than 3 books accessible to the children can be in poor repair. Books that are not in good repair cannot be counted to meet the requirements for the number of books listed in 1.1, 3.1, and 5.1.

3.3. To score "Yes," at least one instance must be observed, or staff report using books daily at another time indicated on their schedule.

5.1. To give credit, none of the books can be violent or frightening.

5.2. A wide selection includes books about people of varying races, ages, and abilities; animals; familiar objects; familiar routines.

5.3. At least 1 instance must be observed to give credit for this indicator.

5.4. This must be observed to give credit. Do not give credit if any book time, for example, a large group story time, is not warm and interactive, even if other, less formal times with books meet the requirement.

7.1. An area cannot be considered a book area if many toys and materials other than books are included.

7.2. Several instances must be observed throughout the observation.

7.3. To give credit, books must be added or changed at least monthly.

Questions

7.3. Do you add to or change the books that are put out for the children to use? *If yes, ask:* How often do you do this? What kinds of books are added?

Inadequate		Minimal		Good		Excellent
1	2	3	4	5	6	7

ACTIVITIES

15. Fine motor

1.1 No appropriate fine motor materials accessible for daily use.*

1.2 Materials are generally in poor repair.

3.1 Some appropriate fine motor materials accessible for daily use.*

3.2 Materials are accessible for much of the day.

3.3 Materials generally in good repair.*

5.1 Many and varied appropriate fine motor materials accessible for much of the day.*

5.2 Materials are well-organized (Ex. similar toys stored together; sets of toys in separate containers; toys picked up, sorted, and restored as needed).

7.1 Materials rotated to provide variety.*

7.2 Materials of different levels of difficulty accessible (Ex. some challenging and some easy for all children in group, including those with disabilities).*

---

*Notes for Clarification

1.1. Score "Yes" if there are fewer than three intact, usable examples of fine motor materials accessible for some time during the day.

1.1, 3.1, 5.1. Examples of appropriate fine motor materials:

- Infants—grasping toys, busy boxes, nested cups, containers to fill and dump, textured toys, cradle gyms.
- Toddlers—shape sorting games, large stringing beads, big pegs with peg boards, simple puzzles, pop beads, stacking rings, nesting toys, medium or large interlocking blocks, crayons.

3.1. To give credit, at least five intact, usable examples of fine motor toys must be accessible during some part of a 3-hour observation.

3.3. "Generally" means 80% of fine motor materials.

5.1. "Many" means no fewer than 10 toys for a group of 5 infants or 15 toys for a group of 5 toddlers, and at least 1 additional toy for each child over that number in each age group. The observer should carefully examine materials to ensure they match the children's abilities—challenging but not frustrating—and give credit only for such materials. "Varied" means materials that require different skills (such as grasping, shaking, turning, pushing, pulling, poking, putting together, using thumb and forefinger together, scribbling). Materials should also vary in color, size, shape, texture, sound, and action.

7.1. To give credit, materials must be rotated at least monthly.

7.2. To give credit, there must be at least two examples of materials of different levels of difficulty.

Questions

7.1. Do you have any additional fine motor materials that you use with the children? *If yes, ask:* Could you please show them to me?

16. Active physical play*

1.1 No appropriate outdoor or indoor space used regularly for active physical play.*

1.2 No appropriate equipment/materials.*

1.3 Equipment/materials generally in poor repair.

3.1 Open space provided indoors for active physical play much of day (Ex. young infants can move freely on carpet; children can crawl and walk around).*

3.2 Some space for outdoor physical play used by infants/toddlers at least 3 times a week, year-round, except in very bad weather.*

3.3 Some appropriate materials and equipment used daily; materials/equipment generally in good repair.*

5.1 Easily accessible outdoor area where infants/toddlers are separated from older children is used at least 1 hour daily year-round, except in very bad weather.*

5.2 Large active play area that is not crowded or cluttered.*

5.3 Ample materials and equipment for physical activity so children have access without long periods of waiting.

5.4 Some equipment that can be used by each child in the group, including child with disabilities, if enrolled.

5.5 All space and equipment is appropriate for children.*

7.1 Outdoor space has 2 or more types of surfaces permitting different types of play (Ex. grass, outdoor carpet, rubber cushioning surface, decking).*

7.2 Outdoor area has some protection from the elements (Ex. shade in summer; sun in winter; wind break; good drainage).*

7.3 Materials used daily stimulate a variety of large muscle skills (Ex. crawling, walking, balancing, climbing, ball play).*

(See Notes for Clarification and Questions on next page)

*Notes for Clarification

Item 16. Active physical play requires that the children be active in order to develop their gross motor skills. Taking children for rides in strollers, swinging them in swings, or having them play in the sandbox should not be counted as active physical play. Non-mobile babies should be allowed to move freely to the extent that they are able, for example on a blanket or other safe surface. Children who can crawl or walk should be given developmentally appropriate opportunities to practice gross motor skills. In this item, the terms "equipment" and "materials" are used interchangeably.

1.1. If neither indoor nor outdoor space is used for active physical play, score 1.1 "Yes."

1.1, 1.2, 3.3, 5.5. Appropriate indoor and outdoor spaces and equipment/ materials must be safe for infants and toddlers. For example, cushioning surfaces in fall zones must be adequate; equipment should not allow falls from high places; no sharp edges, splinters, protrusions, or entrapment hazards.

1.2, 3.3, 5.5. Examples of appropriate materials and equipment:

- Infants—outdoor pad or blanket, crib gym for younger infants, small push toys, balls, sturdy things to pull up on, ramps for crawling
- Toddlers—riding toys without pedals, large push-pull wheel toys, balls and bean bags, age-appropriate climbing equipment, slide, balance board, cushions or rugs for tumbling, tunnels, large cardboard boxes

3.1. If any child is confined to a space that severely restricts active physical movement for long periods (e.g., 30 minutes or more), do not give credit. For example, score "No" if a child is kept in a swing, infant seat, or large group activity with no option for using the active play space for long periods.

3.2. Children should be dressed properly and taken outdoors to play except on those *relatively few* days of very bad weather.

5.1. The outdoor space must be easily accessible to the adults and children currently a part of the program. Access should be considered for both typically developing children and those with disabilities, if enrolled. Access requirements will differ based on abilities of children enrolled and of adults who are part of the regular program. Two-year-olds do not need to be separated from preschoolers to give credit, unless safety or access to appropriate active physical experiences, due to the presence of older children, is an issue.

Programs operating for at least 8 hours/day must have 1 hour of access to outdoor active physical play space daily. Less time is required for programs operating less than 8 hours a day. See Explanation of Terms, p. 7, for time required for shorter programs.

5.2. If there are 2 or more active play areas used with the children, score this indicator based on the average of what children experience. For example, if the indoor play area is small and crowded and it is used substantially more than an uncluttered, spacious outdoor space, do not give credit. If the opposite is true, then credit should be given.

7.1. At least 1 firm and 1 soft play surface must be accessible daily outdoors. Do not give credit for space within a fall zone as a soft play surface.

7.2. Only 1 example of protection from the elements must be observed, but the protection must match the most prevalent adverse conditions caused by the elements in the local area.

7.3. To meet the requirement for a "variety of skills," there should be 7–9 different skills that are obviously encouraged by the equipment/materials children can use. Consider both stationary and portable equipment.

Questions

1.1, 3.1, 3.2, 5.1. Are any areas used by this group for active physical play, including space indoors and outdoors? *If yes, and not observed, ask:* Could you please show me these areas? How often are they used, and for about how long?

Inadequate		Minimal		Good		Excellent
1	2	3	4	5	6	7

17. Art*

1.1 No appropriate art materials provided for use by children.*

1.2 Toxic or unsafe materials are used for art (Ex. shaving cream, glitter, permanent markers, acrylic or oil paints, things children can choke on such as styrofoam peanuts or small beads).*

3.1 Some art materials used with children at least once a week.* *NA permitted.*

3.2 All art materials used with children are non-toxic, safe, and appropriate.*

3.3 Children not required to participate; alternative activities available.*

5.1 Younger toddlers offered some art 3 times a week; older toddlers offered art daily.* *NA permitted.*

5.2 Individual expression encouraged (Ex. expectations based on children's abilities; children not asked to copy an example; coloring books and ditto pages not used).*

5.3 Staff facilitate appropriate use of materials (Ex. tape paper in place for scribbling; use adaptive equipment when needed; encourage children to paint on paper and not to eat paint).

7.1 A variety of materials is introduced as children are ready (Ex. crayons and watercolor markers for the youngest children; paints, play dough added for older toddlers and twos).*

7.2 Access to materials is based on children's abilities (Ex. made available with close supervision for younger children; very simple materials, such as large crayons or large chalk accessible to 2-year-olds).

Notes for Clarification

Item 17. Mark this item NA if all children in group are younger than 12 months of age. However, if art activities are used with infants, then the item must be scored and specified indicators (3.1, 5.1) will be scored NA.

1.1, 3.2. Examples of appropriate art materials: crayons, water color markers, brush and finger paints, play dough, collage materials of different textures. Only the simplest materials should be used with younger toddlers. Other materials should be added as children gain skills and ability to use materials appropriately.

All materials must be non-toxic and safe. Score this item based only on the art materials used with the children. Edible materials (such as chocolate pudding, dried pasta, pop corn, and so forth) can not be counted as art materials because they give a misleading message about the proper use of food. The possible health (sanitary issues), safety (e.g., choking hazards), and supervision consequences of using food in art should be considered in Items 10, 11, and 25.

1.2. Score "Yes" if *any* toxic or unsafe art materials are ever used by children, even if most materials used are non-toxic and safe.

3.1. "Some" means at least 1 usable example (e.g., crayons with paper).

3.3. There must be at least 2 other activities available that children can choose to do without a negative response from the staff.

5.1. "Younger toddlers" are children 12–23 months of age; "older toddlers" are children 24–30 months of age.

5.2. To give credit, all art activities used with children should encourage individual expression.

7.1. To give credit, "younger toddlers" must be offered at least 3 different art materials at some time during the week. "Older toddlers" must have access to more than 3 different materials on a weekly basis, and there must be variation within each material. To score, consider art materials accessible during the observation, children's art on display, and staff report.

Questions

1.2, 3.2. Are art materials used with the children? *If yes, ask:* What materials are used? May I see these art supplies? Are edible materials ever used for art?

3.1, 5.1. How often are art materials used with the children?

7.1. How do you choose what art materials to offer the children?

Inadequate		Minimal		Good		Excellent
1	2	3	4	5	6	7

18. Music and movement

1.1 No music/movement experiences for children.*

1.2 Loud music is on much of the day and interferes with ongoing activities (Ex. constant background music makes conversation in normal tones difficult; music raises noise level).*

3.1 Some musical materials, toys, or instruments accessible for free play daily, for much of the day (Ex. rattles, chime toy, music box, xylophone, drum).*

3.2 Staff initiate at least 1 music activity daily (Ex. sing songs with children; soft music turned on at naptime; play music for dancing).

3.3 Children not required to participate in group music activities; alternative activities available.*

5.1 Many pleasant sounding musical toys and/or instruments accessible daily, for much of the day.*

5.2 Staff informally sing/chant daily with children.*

5.3 In addition to singing, staff provide other music experience daily (Ex. tape or CD used; guitar played for children; music used for nap or dancing).

5.4 Recorded music is used at limited times and with a positive purpose (Ex. quiet music at nap; put on for dancing or singing).*

7.1 Musical toys or instruments rotated to provide variety.*

7.2 Various types of music are used with children (Ex. classical and popular; music characteristic of different cultures; songs sung in different languages).*

7.3 Staff encourage children to dance, clap, or sing along (Ex. dance to music while holding baby; clap to rhythm with toddlers; participate with children).*

---

*Notes for Clarification

1.1. Examples of materials for use in music/movement experiences: record/tape/CD player; variety of records, tapes, CDs; music boxes; musical toys and instruments; safe, home-made musical instruments such as shakers made of plastic bottles filled with sand or pebbles, with caps securely fastened. Score "Yes" if children do not have a music/movement experience at least once a day.

1.2. Score "Yes" if loud music is on for most of a 3-hour observation.

3.1. "Some" means at least 2 safe musical materials, toys, or instruments are accessible.

3.3. To give credit, there must be more than 1 alternative activity available for children to choose during group music activities.

5.1. "Many" means at least 10 musical toys, but no less than 1 toy per child based on maximum daily attendance permitted. Music materials that are unsafe (e.g., with sharp edges or small removable parts) are not counted to meet the required number. Any safety concerns should also be considered in Item 11, Safety.

5.2. To give credit, this indicator must be observed at least once.

5.4. Credit cannot be given if music is used for long periods (e.g., 20 minutes) as background sound, even if it was originally put on for a specific purpose, such as for children to dance to.

7.1. To give credit, at least 2 music toys or instruments must be rotated monthly.

7.2. To give credit, at least 3 different types of music must be used regularly. For any music to be counted as an example of a type, it must be appropriate for children; e.g., no violent or sexually explicit content.

7.3. One instance must be observed to give credit.

Questions

3.2, 5.3. Do you use any music with the children? *If yes, ask:* How is this handled? How often is this done?

7.1. Do you have any other musical toys or instruments that the children can use? Could you please show me? How are these used?

7.2. What types of music are used with the children? Can you give me some examples?

Inadequate		Minimal		Good		Excellent
1	2	3	4	5	6	7

19. Blocks*

1.1 No materials available for block play.*

3.1 At least 1 set of blocks (6 or more blocks of the same type) accessible daily.*

3.2 Some accessories for blocks accessible daily.*

3.3 Blocks and accessories accessible much of the day.

5.1 At least 2 sets (10 or more blocks per set) of different types accessible daily for much of the day.*

5.2 Blocks and accessories sorted by type.

5.3 Space used for toddler's block play is out of traffic and has a steady surface.

7.1 At least 3 sets (10 or more blocks per set) of different types accessible daily for much of the day.*

7.2 Variety of accessories including transportation toys, people, animals.*

7.3 Staff do simple block play with children.*

---

*Notes for Clarification

Item 19. Mark this item NA if all children in care are younger than 12 months of age.

1.1, 3.1, 3.2, 5.1, 7.1. Examples of materials for block play: soft blocks; light-weight blocks of various sizes, shapes, colors; large cardboard blocks; accessories such as containers to fill and dump, toy trucks or cars; people and animals.

   Note that interlocking blocks, such as Duplo, are considered under Item 15. Fine motor, and are not counted here.

3.1, 3.2. Programs operating for at least 8 hours per day must have 1 hour of access to blocks and accessories daily. Less time is required for programs operating less than 8 hours a day. See Explanation of Terms, p. 7, for time required for shorter programs.

3.1, 5.1, 7.1. A "set" of blocks means a group of blocks that is designed to be used together. In determining whether a number of blocks can be considered a "set," they must be of the same type and composition. They may differ in shape, size, and color, but must obviously be designed to be used as a group. Different types of blocks cannot be combined to give credit for 1 set.

3.2. "Some" means at least 5 accessories of different types. To give credit, accessories must be stored near the blocks, or if not, they must be observed being used with blocks during block play.

7.2. "Variety" means at least 5 materials from each of the following categories: transportation toys, people, and animals, resulting in a total of at least 15.

7.3. To give credit, this indicator must be observed at least once.

Inadequate		Minimal		Good		Excellent
1	2	3	4	5	6	7

20. Dramatic play

1.1 No materials accessible for dramatic play.*

3.1 Some age-appropriate dramatic play materials accessible, including dolls and soft animals.*

3.2 Materials accessible daily for much of the day.

5.1 Many and varied age-appropriate dramatic play materials accessible daily.*

5.2 Props represent what children experience in every day life (Ex. household routines, work, transportation).

5.3 Materials are organized by type (Ex. play dishes in separate container; dolls stored together; dress-up hats and purses hung on pegs).

5.4 Some child-sized play furniture for toddlers (Ex. small sink or stove, baby stroller, shopping cart).
NA permitted.

7.1 Props provided to represent diversity (Ex. dolls representing different races/cultures; equipment used by people of different cultures or with disabilities).*

7.2 Props provided for toddlers to use active dramatic play outdoors or in other large area. *NA permitted.*

7.3 Staff pretend with children in play (Ex. talk to child on toy telephone; rock and talk to baby doll).*

Notes for Clarification

1.1, 3.1, 5.1. Examples of materials for dramatic play:
- Infants—dolls, soft animals, pots and pans, toy telephones
- Toddlers—dress-up clothes; child-sized house furniture; cooking/eating equipment such as pots and pans, dishes, spoons; play foods; dolls; doll furnishings; soft animals; small play buildings with accessories; toy telephones

3.1. To give credit, 2 or more dolls and 2 or more soft animals must be accessible to children.

5.1. For infants, "many" requires 3–5 of the examples on the list of materials. For toddlers, 2 or more of each example of toy mentioned in the materials list is required. However, no more than 2 types can be missing, and there must be more of other types if 1 or 2 types are missing.

7.1. To give credit, there must be dolls representing at least 3 different races and at least 2 other examples of materials that show diversity, and all props must be associated with a positive image of the group represented.

7.3. To give credit, this indicator must be observed at least once during the observation.

Inadequate		Minimal		Good		Excellent
1	2	3	4	5	6	7

21. Sand and water play*

1.1 Sand or water play not available for children 18 months or older.

3.1 Some sand or water play provided outdoors or indoors at least once every 2 weeks.

3.2 Close supervision of sand/water play.*

3.3 Some toys used for sand/water play.*

5.1 Sand or water play at least once a week.

5.2 Variety of toys used for sand/water play.*

5.3 Sand or water activities set up to facilitate play (Ex. enough sand/water for play; not too crowded for toys; enough space for number of children participating).

7.1 Sand or water play provided daily.

7.2 Different activities done with sand or water (Ex. on different days water used for washing dolls, floating toys, and pouring).*

---

*Notes for Clarification

Item 21. Mark this item NA if all children in care are younger than 18 months of age. The possible health, safety, and supervision consequences of using sand or water with children under 18 months of age should be considered in Items 10, 11, and 25.

In addition to sand, other fine-grained materials that can easily be used for digging and pouring, such as sterilized potting soil or very finely shredded mulch, may be counted. Materials that pose a danger to children of this age, such as dried beans, small pebbles, styrofoam chips, corn meal, and flour, cannot be counted as a substitute for sand.

Water play can be provided by using materials such as a running hose, sprinkler, dishpans, or a water table.

Sand and water play require action on the part of the staff to provide appropriate materials for such activity. Allowing children to play in puddles or dig in dirt on the playground does not meet the requirements for this item.

3.2. Score "No" if there are any instances observed of children drinking water used for play, eating sand, throwing sand or water in a way that hurts or endangers anyone, or children falling on slippery floors in sand/water play area. If sand or water play is not observed, base score on supervision of other activities observed, and teacher response during interview.

3.3. "Some" means at least 2 toys for children to use with sand/water play.

3.3, 5.2. Examples of toys for use with sand and water are: kitchen utensils, shovel and bucket, small cars and trucks, floating toys, plastic containers.

7.2. Give credit if staff report that different activities are used with sand or water at least once a week.

Questions

1.1, 3.1, 5.1, 7.1. Do the children use sand or water? *If yes, ask:* How often is this done?

3.3, 5.2. Are any toys used for the sand and water play? Could you please describe them or show me?

7.2. Are there any other activities or materials used with sand or water in addition to what I saw today? Could you tell me about them?

Inadequate		Minimal		Good		Excellent
1	2	3	4	5	6	7

22. Nature/science

1.1 No pictures, books, or toys that represent nature realistically (Ex. animals only shown as cartoons or fanciful characters).

1.2 No opportunities for children to experience the natural world (Ex. no exposure to trees, grass, or birds; no living plants or pets in room; no seashells or other natural objects).

3.1 Some pictures, books, or toys that represent nature realistically; all are developmentally appropriate (Ex. non-frightening posters clearly showing real animals; realistic toy animals).*

3.2 Materials accessible daily.*

3.3 Some opportunities to experience the natural world daily, either indoors or outdoors.*

5.1 Outdoor experiences with nature provided at least 2 times a week (Ex. infants placed on blanket on grass; toddlers explore flowers and trees in yard or park; children taken for stroller ride where staff point out natural things).*

5.2 Some daily experiences with living plants or animals indoors (Ex. plant in the room to look at; staff point out trees, flowers, or birds from window; children visit aquarium).

5.3 Everyday events used as a basis for learning about nature/science (Ex. talking about the weather; pointing out insects or birds; blowing bubbles; watching rain or snow fall).*

7.1 Staff show interest in and respect for nature (Ex. are caring with pets; help children handle natural things carefully; take children outside in different kinds of weather).

7.2 Nature/science materials are well-organized and in good repair (Ex. collections stored in separate containers; animal cages clean).

Notes for Clarification

3.1. "Some" means at least 2 nature/science pictures, books, or toys.

3.2. Programs operating for 8 hours/day or more must have 1 hour of access to nature/science materials daily. Less time is required for programs operating less than 8 hours a day. See "Explanation of Terms" on p. 7 for time required in shorter programs. To count as accessible, children must be able to reach and use the books/toys, and easily see the pictures.

3.3. The intent of this indicator is that children are given opportunities to interact with nature. This can occur either by taking children outside to see or experience natural things such as trees, grass, and birds, or by providing experiences with nature indoors, such as through living plants, an aquarium, classroom pets, and watching birds at a window feeder. "Some" means that more than 1 opportunity exists daily.

5.1. To give credit for this indicator, the outdoor experiences children have must include living plants and/or animals.

5.3. To give credit, at least 1 instance must be observed.

Questions

5.1. How often are children taken outdoors? Could you describe any experiences they have with nature when they are outdoors?

Inadequate		Minimal		Good		Excellent
1	2	3	4	5	6	7

23. Use of TV, video, and/or computer*

1.1 Materials used are not developmentally appropriate (Ex. violent, sexually explicit content, frightening characters or stories, too difficult).*

1.2 No alternative activity is allowed while TV/video/computer being used (Ex. all children must watch video at same time).

1.3 Television, video, and/or computer used with children under 12 months of age.*
NA permitted.

3.1 All materials used are developmentally appropriate, non-violent, and culturally sensitive.

3.2 At least 1 alternative activity accessible while TV/video/computer is used (Ex. children do not have to sit in front of TV and may go to other activity).

3.3 Time allowed for children over 12 months of age to use TV/video or computer is limited (Ex. TV/video limited to 30 minutes a day in a full-day program; each computer turn is limited to 10 minutes).*

5.1 Materials used are limited to those considered "good for children" (Ex. simple stories, music and dance, very simple computer games, but not most cartoons).

5.2 Many alternative activities accessible for free choice while TV/video/computer is used.*

5.3 Staff are actively involved in use of TV, video, or computer (Ex. watch and discuss video with children; do activity suggested in educational TV program; help children learn to use computer appropriately).

7.1 Most of the materials encourage active involvement (Ex. children can dance, sing, or exercise to video; computer software interests children).

7.2 Materials used to support and extend children's current interests and experiences (Ex. video on snowman on snowy day; video showing children's everyday experiences).

---

*Notes for Clarification

Item 23. Since infants and toddlers learn primarily through interactions and hands-on experiences with the real world, use of TV, video, and computer is not required. If TV, video, and computers are not used, score the item NA. If not observed, ask about the use of TV, video, and computers as they are often shared by several classes and may not be evident during the observation time.

Since new audiovisual media products are constantly being developed, consider all audiovisual materials or equipment used with the children, even if not named explicitly. For example, DVD materials and electronic games would be considered in scoring. Use of radio programs is also considered here.

1.1. Score "Yes" if *any* inappropriate material is ever used including materials containing violent, frightening, or sexually explicit content.

1.3, 3.3. Use with children under 12 months of age results in a score of 1. Any use with toddlers should be limited.

5.2. Three or more alternative activities must be accessible while TV or computer is used.

Questions

1.1, 3.1, 5.1, 7.1. Are TV, videos, computers, or other audiovisual materials used with the children? *If yes, ask:* How are they used? How do you choose the materials?

1.2. Are other activities accessible to the children while the TV or videos are used?

3.3. How often are TV, video, or computers used with the children? For what length of time are these available?

5.3. How do you supervise when children watch TV or use the computer?

7.1. Do any of the materials encourage active involvement by the children? Please give some examples.

7.2. Do you use TV, video, and computer materials that relate to classroom topics or other things that the children are interested in? Please explain.

Inadequate		Minimal		Good		Excellent
1	2	3	4	5	6	7

24. Promoting acceptance of diversity*

1.1 No evidence of racial or cultural diversity observed in materials.*

1.2 Materials showing diversity present only negative stereotypes (Ex. races, cultures, ages, abilities, or gender shown negatively).

1.3 Staff demonstrate prejudice against others (Ex. against child or other adult from different race or cultural group; against person with disability).

3.1 At least 3 examples of racial or cultural diversity observed in materials (Ex. multiracial or multicultural dolls, books, pictures; music tapes or CDs from several cultures; in bilingual areas some materials accessible in children's primary language).*

3.2 Materials show diversity in a positive way.

3.3 No prejudice is shown *or* staff intervene appropriately to counteract prejudice shown by children or other adults (Ex. explain similarities and differences; establish rules for fair treatment of others).

5.1 Many books, pictures, and materials showing diversity (Ex. people of different races, cultures, ages, abilities, and gender in non-stereotyping roles).*

5.2 Dolls representing at least 3 races accessible (Ex. skin tones or facial features).*

7.1 Non-sexist images in pictures or books accessible to children (Ex. men and women, boys and girls in similar work or play roles).

7.2 Cultural awareness shown in a variety of activities (Ex. various types of music, celebration of different holidays and customs, ethnic foods served).*

---

*Notes for Clarification

Item 24. When assessing diversity in materials, consider all areas and materials used by children, including displayed pictures and photos, books, puzzles, games, dolls, play people used with blocks, puppets, music tapes or CDs, computer software, videos.

1.1. To score "No," there must be at least 2 examples of materials that show racial or cultural diversity, that are obvious to the children, in the room used most of the time by them. 1 poster showing children of many races is counted as 1 example; 2 baby dolls of different races also count as 1 example.

3.1, 5.1. If materials are difficult to find or observe, do not give credit for 3.1 and 5.1.

5.1. To give credit, the observer must find a total of 10 different examples, some in the books, some in pictures, and some in materials (excluding dolls that are required in 5.2). All examples must be easily experienced by children. These 10 examples must include at least 4 of the 5 types of diversity (races, cultures, ages, abilities, and gender) listed as examples in the indicator.

5.1, 5.2. Small dolls, used, for example, with a doll house or for block play, count as dolls for these indicators. Puppets count as materials, but not as dolls.

7.2. To give credit, the representation of various cultures in accessible materials throughout the classroom must be observed, and staff must report at least one routine or special activity that reflects awareness of cultural diversity if such an activity was not observed.

Questions

7.2. Are there any activities used to help children become aware of diversity? *If yes, ask:* Can you give some examples?

INTERACTION

25. Supervision of play and learning*

1.1 Insufficient supervision to protect children's safety (Ex. staff often leave children and can not see, hear, or reach them; children unattended in dangerous situation).*

3.1 Children are within sight, hearing, and easy reach of staff with no more than a few momentary lapses (Ex. staff quickly get materials from closet in room; staff call into building from door while supervising children on playground).*

3.2 Attention is on caregiving responsibilities, not on other tasks or interests.

5.1 Staff show awareness of the whole group even while working with 1 child or a small group.

5.2 Staff react quickly to solve problems in a comforting and supportive way.

5.3 Staff play with children and show interest in or appreciation of what they do.*

5.4 Staff give children help and encouragement when needed (Ex. help child who is wandering to get involved in play; help baby access toy on shelf).

7.1 Staff watch carefully and usually act to avoid problems before they occur (Ex. bring out duplicate toys; move active play before it disrupts quiet play).

7.2 Supervision is individualized (Ex. closer supervision of child with greater needs; infant moved to avoid boredom).

7.3 Staff vary supervision to meet differing requirements of activities (Ex. art activities and materials with small pieces closely supervised).

Notes for Clarification

Item 25. For this item consider both indoor and outdoor supervision. To score this item for outdoor supervision where several groups are being supervised together, consider: all teachers supervising gross motor activities; all children of similar age/abilities as those in group you are observing; numbers of adults and children; whether adults are supervising the most hazardous areas/activities adequately. Since supervision of the various personal care routines is handled in the individual items, it is not considered here (see Items 7. Meals/snacks, 8. Nap, and 9. Diapering/toileting).

1.1, 3.1. A "momentary lapse in supervision" means that staff are in the space used by the children but cannot see, hear, or reach children, or are not attending to children for a period of less than 1 minute. No momentary lapse in supervision can occur when the risk of danger is high. If there are only a few momentary lapses in supervision, do not score Indicator 1.1 "Yes." However, if there are many momentary lapses, 1 lapse when the risk is high, or 1 lapse in supervision of over 1 minute, where staff cannot easily see, hear, and reach a child at all, score Indicator 1.1 "Yes."

3.1. "Few" means no more than 5 momentary lapses during a 3-hour observation. However, not even 1 momentary lapse in supervision can occur when risk of danger is high, such as while children are on a diapering table, using climbing equipment, or participating in water play.

5.3. It must be evident throughout the observation that a significant amount of time is spent in playing with the children and showing interest in and appreciation of children's play. If the vast majority of staff time is taken up in routine care, credit cannot be given, even if staff play with the children for some portion of the observation.

Inadequate		Minimal		Good		Excellent
1	2	3	4	5	6	7

26. Peer interaction

1.1 Little or no appropriate peer interaction possible (Ex. children separated in cribs, swings, or highchairs while awake; toddlers crowded into small space with few toys).

1.2 Negative peer interaction either ignored or handled harshly.*

3.1 Peer interaction is possible much of the day (Ex. non-mobile infants have supervised play near others; toddlers allowed to form natural groupings).

3.2 Staff usually stop negative peer interaction (Ex. stop hitting, biting, grabbing toys).*

5.1 Staff facilitate positive peer interactions among all children (Ex. place infants where they can watch and react to others; help toddlers find duplicate toys; include child with disability in play with others).

5.2 Staff model positive social interaction (Ex. warm and affectionate; use gentle touching; polite to children and not "bossy").*

7.1 Staff explain children's actions, intentions, and feelings to other children (Ex. help children recognize facial expressions of sadness or joy; explain that other child did not mean any harm; praise child for getting own duplicate toy).*

7.2 Staff point out and talk about instances of positive social interaction among children or between adults and children (Ex. help children notice comforting; smile and talk to baby who notices other children; praise 2-year-olds for working together to bring chairs to table).*

Notes for Clarification

1.2. If no negative peer interaction is observed, score this indicator "No."

3.2. Staff must stop mildly negative peer interactions at least 75% of the time to give credit, and all major problems in which children are being hurt. In addition, the intervention can not ever be harsh to give credit. If no negative peer interaction is observed, score this indicator "Yes."

5.2. To give credit, no staff member can be observed modeling negative social skills with the children or with other adults.

7.1. At least 2 instances must be observed during the first 3 hours of observation to give credit for this indicator.

7.2. At least 1 instance must be observed during the first 3 hours of observation to give credit for this indicator.

| Inadequate | | Minimal | | Good | | Excellent |
| 1 | 2 | 3 | 4 | 5 | 6 | 7 |

27. Staff-child interaction*

1.1 Interaction is impersonal or negative (Ex. staff rarely respond to, smile at, talk to, or listen to children).

1.2 Uneven amount of positive attention given to children (Ex. staff have favorite child who gets far more attention than others).

1.3 Physical contact is not warm or responsive, or is harsh.

3.1 Occasional smiling, talking, and affection shown to children throughout the day.*

3.2 Staff usually respond sympathetically to help children who are hurt, angry, or upset.*

3.3 No harsh verbal or physical staff-child interaction.

3.4 Some warm and responsive physical affection throughout the day in routines or play (Ex. hold child gently while reading a book; cuddle child during bottle feeding).

5.1 Frequent positive staff-child interaction throughout the day (Ex. initiate verbal and physical play; respond when child initiates interactions; show delight in child's activity).*

5.2 Staff and children usually relaxed, voices pleasant, frequent smiling.*

5.3 Much holding, patting, and physical warmth shown throughout the day.*

7.1 Interaction is responsive to each child's mood and needs (Ex. soothing with tired child; more active with playful child; reassuring with frightened child).

7.2 Staff are usually sensitive about children's feelings and reactions (Ex. avoid abrupt interruptions, warn baby before picking him or her up).*

---

*Notes for Clarification

Item 27. While the indicators for quality in this item generally hold true across a diversity of cultures and individuals, the ways in which they are expressed may differ. For example, direct eye contact in some cultures is a sign of respect; in others, a sign of disrespect. Similarly, some individuals are more likely to smile and be demonstrative than others. However, the requirements of the indicators must be met by staff, although there can be some variation in the way this is done.

3.1. To give credit, the required interactions need not occur frequently, but must occur regularly, during both routines and play, and all children should be recipients of these interactions.

3.2. Sympathetic response means that staff notice and validate a child's feelings, even if the child is showing emotions that are often considered unacceptable, such as anger or impatience. The feelings should be accepted, although inappropriate behaviors, such as hitting or throwing things, should not be allowed. A sympathetic response should be provided in most, but not necessarily all, cases. If children are able to quickly solve minor problems themselves, then teacher response is not needed. The observer needs to get an overall impression of the response of the staff. If minor problems persist and are ignored or if staff responds in a negative manner, give no credit for this indicator.

5.1. To give credit, the required interactions must occur frequently, during both routines and play, and all children should be recipients of these interactions.

5.2. "Usually," in this indicator, means most of the time for each child and for each staff member. The overall tone throughout the observation should be pleasant in both routines and play. Any stress or upset should be resolved quickly.

5.3. Physical warmth must be used appropriately to give credit. This means the contact is pleasant and not intrusive to the children or likely to result in any problems.

7.2. "Usually," in this indicator, means most of the time for each child. Consider both verbal and non-verbal communication when scoring.

Inadequate		Minimal		Good		Excellent
1	2	3	4	5	6	7

28. Discipline

1.1 Discipline is *either* so strict that children are punished or restricted often *or* so lax that there is little order or control.

1.2 Children controlled with severe methods such as spanking, shouting, confining children for long periods, or withholding food.

3.1 Staff never use physical punishment or severe discipline.

3.2 Staff *usually* maintain enough control to prevent problems (Ex. children hurting one another or endangering themselves; being destructive).

3.3 Expectations are generally realistic and based on age and ability of children (Ex. sharing is not forced although it may be talked about; children not expected to wait for long periods).

5.1 Program is set up to avoid conflict and promote appropriate interaction (Ex. duplicate toys accessible; child with favorite toy protected from others; children not crowded; staff respond quickly to problems; smooth transitions).

5.2 Positive methods of discipline used effectively (Ex. redirecting child from negative situation to other activity; time-out rarely used, and never with children under 2 years of age).

5.3 Attention frequently given when children are behaving well (Ex. staff watch, smile, or participate while children are playing, being fed, and so forth).*

5.4 Staff react consistently to children's behavior.

7.1 Staff help children understand the effects of their own actions on others (Ex. call attention to other child's crying face; explain child's anger when her block structure is knocked down).*

7.2 Staff help children learn to use communication rather than aggression to solve problems (Ex. provide words for non-talkers; encourage verbal children to use words).*

7.3 Staff seek advice from other professionals concerning behavior problems.

Notes for Clarification

5.3. "Attention" means showing enjoyment or interest in what children do. Praise for good behavior is not required as part of the attention given.

7.1. To give credit, at least 1 example of an explanation of how a child's behavior affected another person must be observed during the 3-hour observation to demonstrate that it is a regular part of discipline practice. If there are no negative effects of children's actions observed, explanation of positive effects are acceptable to give credit.

7.2. To give credit, at least 1 example of staff helping children learn to use communication rather than aggression to solve problems must be observed. If no aggression is observed, give credit if staff help children use either non-verbal or verbal communication skills with one another in other interpersonal interaction.

Questions

1.1. Do you ever find it necessary to use discipline? Please describe what methods you use.

7.3. What do you do if you have a child whose behavior is extremely difficult to handle? Do you ever ask for help from others? *If yes, ask:* Can you give some examples of who might be asked?

49

Inadequate		Minimal		Good		Excellent
1	2	3	4	5	6	7

PROGRAM STRUCTURE

29. Schedule*

1.1 Schedule is *either* too rigid, not satisfying needs of many children, *or* too flexible (chaotic), lacking a dependable sequence of daily events.*

1.2 Children's routine needs are not met (Ex. crying children, rushed mealtimes, delays in diapering).*

1.3 Staff have no time to supervise children at play (Ex. all time taken up with routines).

3.1 Schedule meets the needs of most of the children.

3.2 Staff provide play activities as part of the daily schedule.*

5.1 Schedule for basic routines is flexible and individualized to meet each child's needs (Ex. infants on individual schedules; tired toddler can have early nap).*

5.2 Schedule provides balance of indoor and outdoor activities.*

5.3 Active and quiet play varied to meet children's needs.

5.4 No long periods of waiting during transitions between daily events.*

7.1 Staff adjust schedule of play activities throughout the day to meet varying needs of children (Ex. change activity if children lose interest; extend play time when children are interested).

7.2 Most transitions between daily events are smooth (Ex. play materials for next activity set out before activity begins; children allowed to eat right after handwashing; transitions done gradually with no more than a few children at a time).

---

*Notes for Clarification

Item 29. "Schedule" means the sequence of daily events experienced by the children. Base score on the actual sequence of events observed rather than on a posted schedule.

1.1. "Daily events" refers to time for indoor and outdoor play activities as well as routines such as meals/snacks, nap/rest, diapering/toileting, and greeting/departing.

1.2. This indicator is true (score "Yes") if any one of the routine care needs (feeding, nap, or diapering/toileting) is not carried out 75% of the time for all children, or if most of the routine needs of any one child are consistently ignored.

3.2. To give credit, the schedule experienced by the children must provide play opportunities where all children are actively involved for much of the day. Passive group gatherings where children are required to listen to the teacher or watch TV, and non-play tasks such as coloring ditto sheets are not given credit. Routines, even if they are done playfully, are also not given credit.

5.1. If the schedule for routines causes difficulties or distress for any child, do not give credit.

5.2. Balance depends on ages of children, their needs and moods, and the weather. All children should have some outdoor time daily, weather permitting. Outdoor time can include quiet, as well as active, experiences.

5.4. Score "No" if children have to wait with nothing to do for more than 3 minutes, or if the waiting time results in obvious distress or problems for children.

Questions

5.1. What do you do if a toddler seems tired before naptime or hungry before mealtime? Is flexibility possible in nap or meal times? *If yes, ask:* How would that be handled?

Inadequate		Minimal		Good		Excellent
1	2	3	4	5	6	7

30. Free play*

1.1 *Either* little opportunity for free play *or* much of the day spent in unsupervised free play.

1.2 Inadequate toys, materials, and equipment provided for children to use in free play (Ex. very few toys or toys generally in poor repair).

3.1 Free play occurs daily, indoors *and* outdoors, weather permitting.*

3.2 Some supervision provided to protect children's safety and to facilitate play.*

3.3 Adequate toys, materials, and equipment accessible for free play.

5.1 Free play occurs for much of the day, both indoors and outdoors, weather permitting.*

5.2 Staff actively involved in facilitating children's play throughout the day (Ex. help children get materials they need; help children use materials that are hard to manage).

5.3 Ample and varied toys and materials and much equipment provided for free play.

7.1 Supervision used as an educational interaction (Ex. staff add words to children's actions; point out interesting features of toys).*

7.2 Staff add materials to stimulate interest during free play (Ex. bring out toys not used earlier that day; rotate materials; do new activity with children).*

---

*Notes for Clarification

Item 30. "Free play" means that the child is permitted to select materials and companions and, as far as possible, to manage play independently. Adult interaction is in response to child's needs. Non-mobile children will have to be offered materials for their free choice and moved to different areas to facilitate access.

3.1. Programs operating for at least 8 hours/day must have 1 hour of free play daily. Less time is required for programs operating less than 8 hours a day. See "Explanation of Terms" on p. 7 for time required for shorter programs.

3.1, 5.1. See "Explanation of Terms" on p. 8 for definition of "weather permitting."

3.2. Score "No" only when supervision is extremely lax.

7.1. At least 2 instances must be observed during the observation.

7.2. To give credit, new materials or experiences must be added to the free play opportunities at least once a month.

Questions

7.2. Do you have any additional play materials for children to use? *If yes, ask:* How often do you change the materials in the room?

31. Group play activities*

1.1 Children must often participate in staff-directed activities, even when not interested (Ex. all do art project at same time; forced to sit in story group).*

1.2 Activities done in groups are usually inappropriate for children (Ex. content too difficult; children not interested; activity lasts too long).

1.3 Staff often behave negatively when children do not participate well in group (Ex. get angry; send child to time-out).*

3.1 Children never forced to participate in group play activities (Ex. children allowed to leave group when they wish and do something else).

3.2 Activities done in group are usually appropriate.

3.3 Staff are usually positive and acceptant with children during group time.*

5.1 Staff are flexible and adjust activity as children join or leave the group (Ex. enough materials for all who want to join; make more space for newcomers; stop activity when children's interest is gone).

5.2 Size of group is appropriate for age and ability of children (Ex. 2–3 infants; 2–5 toddlers; 4–6 two-year-olds).*

5.3 Alternative activities are accessible for children not participating in group.*

7.1 Group activities are set up to maximize children's success (Ex. enough space so children are not crowded; active participation encouraged; book large enough so all can easily see).

7.2 Staff meet the needs of individual children to encourage participation (Ex. child who is distracted cuddled in teacher's lap; signing added for child with hearing difficulty).

***Notes for Clarification**

Item 31. This item refers to play and learning activities, and not to routines. Score this item NA if group play activities are never used. If no group play activity is observed, but there is evidence that such activities are used with the children (e.g., circle time is listed on the displayed schedule, a group activity is shown on a lesson plan), score the item based on information obtained by questions asked during the staff interview. Group play activities are staff-initiated and have an expectation of child participation. This item does not apply to the less formal group activities that usually occur during free play in which children participate in groups because they are interested in doing the same activity at the same time. Examples of these less formal group activities include a few children looking at a book with a teacher or a few children playing close to one another, doing solitary play with blocks with a teacher supervising.

1.1. "Must often participate" means that children are routinely forced or strongly encouraged to take part in a group activity on a daily basis, even though they show signs of wanting to leave the group, being bored or frustrated, interested in something else, or unhappy. Score "Yes" if this situation is observed, or if there is evidence (such as the posted schedule or teacher report) that such activities are used with children daily, or almost daily. Score "No" if all children participate in an observed group activity with interest, engagement, and obvious enjoyment.

1.3. Score "Yes" if it is observed that *any* staff member responds negatively toward *any* child who does not wish to participate in a group play activity, or who does not meet staff expectations for compliant behavior while in a group play activity.

3.3. "Positive and acceptant" behavior must be observed 75% of the time, with neutral behavior accounting for any other interactions with the children.

5.2. Suggestions for group size are provided in the example for this indicator. However, a group size that works successfully will depend on the characteristics of the children in the group and the nature of the activity being done. If any child is bored, unhappy, or not interested and engaged, due to group size, score "No." If all children are happily interested and engaged, score "Yes," because obviously the size of the group matches the type of activity and the needs of each child.

5.3. To give credit, there must be at least 2 interesting play options available to any child who chooses not to participate in any group play activity.

Questions

If group activities are used, but not observed, ask: Do you ever do activities with groups of children where the children are expected to participate? *If yes, ask:* How are these activities handled? What do you do if a child is not interested or wants to wander off? What kinds of activities are done at this time? About how long would the activity last?

Inadequate		Minimal		Good		Excellent
1	2	3	4	5	6	7

32. Provisions for children with disabilities*

1.1 No attempt by staff to assess children's needs or find out about available assessments.

1.2 No attempt to meet children's special needs (Ex. needed modifications not made in teacher interaction, physical environment, program activities, schedule).

1.3 No involvement of parents in helping staff understand children's needs or in setting goals for the children.

1.4 Very little involvement of children with disabilities with the rest of the group (Ex. children do not eat at same table; wander and do not participate in activities).

3.1 Staff have information from available assessments.

3.2 Minor modifications made to meet the needs of children with disabilities.*

3.3 Some involvement of parents and classroom staff in setting goals (Ex. parents and teacher attend Individual Family Service Plan meeting).

3.4 Some involvement of children with disabilities in ongoing activities with the other children.

5.1 Staff follow through with activities and interactions recommended by other professionals (Ex. medical doctors, therapists, educators) to help children meet identified goals.

5.2 Modifications made as needed in environment, program, and schedule so that children can participate in many activities with others.

5.3 Parents frequently involved in sharing information with staff, setting goals, and giving feedback about how program is working.*

7.1 Most of the professional intervention is carried out within the regular activities of the classroom.*

7.2 Children with disabilities are integrated into the group and participate in most activities.

7.3 Staff contribute to individual assessments and intervention plans.

Notes for Clarification

Item 32. This item should be used only if a child with an identified disability is included in the program. Otherwise, score this item NA.

3.2. "Minor modifications" to allow the children to attend may include limited changes in the environment (such as a ramp), schedule, or activities, or adding periodic visits by a therapist to work with the children.

5.3. To give credit, daily (or almost daily) informal communication is required, and formal meetings should take place at least twice a year.

7.1. Credit can be given when either specialists or classroom staff carry out the prescribed intervention within the regular classroom activities.

Questions

Could you describe how you try to meet the needs of the children with disabilities in your group?

1.1, 3.1. Do you have any information from assessments on the children? How is it used?

1.2, 3.2, 5.2. Do you need to do anything special to meet the needs of the children? Please describe what you do.

1.3, 3.3, 5.3. Are you and the children's parents involved in helping to decide how to meet the children's needs? Please describe.

5.1, 7.1. How are intervention services such as therapy handled?

7.3. Are you involved in the children's assessments or in the development of intervention plans? What is your role?

Inadequate		Minimal		Good		Excellent
1	2	3	4	5	6	7

PARENTS AND STAFF

33. Provisions for parents

1.1 No information concerning program given to parents in writing.

1.2 Parents discouraged from observing or being involved in children's program.

3.1 Parents given administrative information about program in writing (Ex. fees, hours of service, health rules for attendance).*

3.2 Some sharing of child-related information between parents and staff (Ex. informal communication; parent conferences upon request; some parenting materials).

3.3 Some possibilities for parents or other family members to be involved in children's program.*

3.4 Interactions between family members and staff are generally respectful and positive.

5.1 Parents urged to observe in child's group prior to enrollment.

5.2 Parents made aware of philosophy and approaches practiced (Ex. parent handbook; discipline policy; descriptions of activities; parent orientation meeting).*

5.3 Much sharing of child-related information between parents and staff (Ex. frequent informal communication; periodic conferences for all children; parent meetings; newsletters; parenting information available on health, safety, and child development).

5.4 Variety of alternatives used to encourage family involvement in children's program (Ex. bring birthday treat; eat lunch with child; attend family pot luck).

7.1 Parents asked for an evaluation of the program annually (Ex. parent questionnaires; group evaluation meetings).

7.2 Parents referred to other professionals when needed (Ex. for special parenting help; for health concerns about child).*

7.3 Parents involved in decision-making roles in program along with staff (Ex. parent representatives on board).

*Notes for Clarification

3.1, 5.2. Materials must be easily understood by all parents. For example, translations provided in languages other than English, if necessary.

3.3. Being "involved" requires active participation on the parents' part, not just sharing information. At least 2 different types of possibilities must be offered to give credit.

7.2. Credit can be given if no referrals have ever been required or made, but, during the teacher interview, staff show that they are well informed and willing to provide this service.

Questions

1.1, 3.1, 5.2. Is any written information about the program given to parents? What is included in this information?

1.2, 3.3, 5.4. Are there any ways that parents can be involved in their child's classroom? Please give some examples.

3.2, 5.3. Do you and the parents share information about the children? How is this done? About how often?

3.4. What is your relationship with the parents usually like?

5.1. Are parents able to visit the class before their child is enrolled? How is this handled?

7.1. Do parents take part in evaluating the program? How is this done? About how often?

7.2. What do you do when parents seem to be having difficulties? *If answer is incomplete, ask:* Do you refer them to other professionals for help?

7.3. Do parents take part in making decisions about the program? How is this handled?

Inadequate		Minimal		Good		Excellent
1	2	3	4	5	6	7

34. Provisions for personal needs of staff

1.1 No special areas for staff (Ex. no separate restroom, lounge, storage for personal belongings).

1.2 No time provided away from children to meet personal needs (Ex. no time for breaks).

3.1 Separate adult restroom.

3.2 Some adult furniture available outside of children's play space.

3.3 Some storage for personal belongings.

3.4 Staff have at least 1 break daily.*

3.5 Accommodation made to meet needs of staff with disabilities currently working in the center. *NA permitted.*

5.1 Lounge with adult-sized furniture available; lounge may have dual use (Ex. office, conference room).

5.2 Convenient storage for personal belongings with security provisions when necessary.*

5.3 Morning, afternoon, and midday "lunch" breaks provided daily.*

5.4 Facilities provided for staff meals/snacks (Ex. refrigerator space; cooking facilities).

5.5 Accommodations made to meet needs of staff with disabilities, even if no one with disabilities is currently employed.*

7.1 Separate adult lounge area (no dual use).

7.2 Comfortable adult furniture in lounge.

7.3 Staff have some flexibility in deciding when to take breaks.

Notes for Clarification

3.4. A minimum of 15 minutes should be provided for a break daily for staff who work an 8-hour day.

5.2. Storage is considered convenient only if it does not require the staff to leave the classroom or neglect the care of the children to get their belongings.

5.3. These requirements are based on an 8-hour work day and should be adjusted for shorter periods. Breaks of 15 minutes in the morning and afternoon, and a 1-hour midday lunch break are required for any staff who work at least 8 hours per day.

5.5. To give credit, the facility and at least one adult restroom must meet the requirements for accessibility stated in the *Notes for Clarification* for Item 1, Indoor space.

Questions

1.2, 3.4, 5.3. Do you get time off during the day when you can be away from the children? *If yes, ask:* When does this happen?

3.3, 5.2. Where do you usually store your belongings, such as your coat or purse? How does this work out?

Inadequate		Minimal		Good		Excellent
1	2	3	4	5	6	7

35. Provisions for professional needs of staff

1.1 No access to phone.*

1.2 No file or storage space for staff materials (Ex. no space to keep materials staff need to prepare activities).

1.3 No space available for individual conferences during hours children are in attendance.

3.1 Convenient access to phone.*

3.2 Access to some file and storage space.

3.3 Some space available for individual conferences during hours children are in attendance.

5.1 Access to ample file and storage space.

5.2 Separate office space used for program administration.*

5.3 Space for conferences and adult group meetings is satisfactory (Ex. dual or shared use does not make scheduling difficult; privacy is assured; adult-sized furniture available).

7.1 Well-equipped office space for program administration (Ex. computer, printer, photocopier, answering machine used).

7.2 Program has space that can be used for individual conferences and group meetings that is conveniently located, comfortable, and separate from space used for children's activities.

Notes for Clarification

1.1. The phone does not have to be located in the classroom, but it must be readily accessible. If the phone is in another building, on another floor, or in a locked office, and not readily accessible, then this indicator is scored "Yes."

3.1. To give credit for this indicator, there must be a phone in the classroom for emergency calls or brief conversations with parents. A cell phone is acceptable if it is accessible.

5.2. To be given credit for this indicator, the office must be on site, open during program hours, and provide administrative services for the program.

Questions

1.1, 3.1. Do you have access to a telephone? Where?

1.2, 3.2, 5.1. Do you have access to any file and storage space? May I see it?

1.3, 3.3, 5.3, 7.2. Is there any space you can use for parent/teacher conferences or for adult group meetings when the children are present? May I see it?

5.2, 7.1. Is there an office for the program? May I see it?

Inadequate		Minimal		Good		Excellent
1	2	3	4	5	6	7

36. Staff interaction and cooperation*

1.1 No communication among staff members of necessary information to meet children's needs (Ex. information regarding early departure of child is not communicated).

1.2 Interpersonal relationships interfere with caregiving responsibilities (Ex. staff socialize instead of looking after children or are curt and angry with one another).

1.3 Staff duties not shared fairly (Ex. one staff member handles most duties, while another is relatively uninvolved).

3.1 Some basic information to meet children's needs is communicated (Ex. all staff know about children's allergies, special feeding instructions, health information).

3.2 Interpersonal interactions among staff do not interfere with caregiving responsibilities.

3.3 Staff duties are shared fairly.

5.1 Child-related information is communicated daily among staff (Ex. information about how routines and play activities are going for specific children).

5.2 Staff interactions are positive and add a feeling of warmth and support.

5.3 Responsibilities are shared so both care and play activities are handled smoothly.

7.1 At least every other week, staff, working with the same group or in the same room, have regular planning time together, when they are not responsible for care of children.

7.2 Responsibilities of each staff member are clearly defined (Ex. one sets out play materials while the other greets children; one prepares for rest while the other finishes lunch supervision).

7.3 Program promotes positive interactions among staff members (Ex. by organizing social events; by encouraging group attendance at professional meetings).*

*Notes for Clarification

Item 36. Score if 2 or more staff members work with the group being observed, even if they work with the same group at different times. Score this item NA if there is only 1 staff member with the group.

7.3. Credit can be given if classroom staff report that the administration encourages some social event at least 2 times a year.

Questions

1.1, 3.1, 5.1. Do you have a chance to share information about the children with the other staff members who work with your group? When and how often does this happen? What kinds of things do you talk about?

7.1. Do you have any planning time with your co-teacher(s)? About how often?

7.2. How do you and your co-teacher(s) decide what each of you will do?

7.3. Does the program ever organize events that you and other staff participate in together? Could you give me some examples? How often is this done?

Inadequate		Minimal		Good		Excellent
1	2	3	4	5	6	7

37. Staff continuity

1.1 Children must adjust to many staff members without a stable person to care for them (Ex. children frequently moved from group to group with different staff members; many different staff members work with 1 group; much coming and going of staff).*

1.2 Most children are changed to new groups more than twice a year (Ex. children moved from infant to pre-toddler to toddler groups within 1 year; groups frequently reorganized to meet ratio and enrollment requirements).

1.3 Transitions to new groups or staff members are abrupt with no preparation for children (Ex. no time to meet new staff members before change; no time to ease into new schedule or room).

1.4 Frequent use of substitutes who do not know the children or the program.*

3.1 Continuity provided by 1–2 stable staff members who lead the group every day (Ex. lead teacher usually present with a number of different helpers; lead teacher and assistant arrange schedules so one is always present).

3.2 Children rarely changed to new groups or staff members more than twice a year.

3.3 Some provision to ease children's transitions to new groups or staff members.

3.4 Substitutes who do not know the children and the program are rarely, if ever, left in charge of the group.

5.1 Very few people (2–3) work with the children in addition to the stable staff (Ex. number of volunteers or students is limited; same "floater" is used consistently with the group).

5.2 Children usually remain with 1 staff member and the same group for at least a year.

5.3 Orientation to new group or staff member occurs gradually, and with a familiar adult present (Ex. familiar teacher goes with child to new group for short play times over several weeks; parent visits new class with child; newly hired staff work with group before familiar staff leave).

5.4 A stable group of substitutes, familiar with children and program, is always available.

7.1 A small group of children is primarily cared for by 1 designated staff member (Ex. most routines carried out by child's favorite staff member; child's primary caregiver plans activities for child and communicates with parents).

7.2 Option is available for child to remain with same staff and group for more than 1 year.

7.3 Enough staff are employed so that only staff members are used as substitutes (Ex. "floaters" available to serve as substitutes without compromising ratios).

Notes for Clarification

1.1. If there is not at least 1 stable person who cares for the children for more than 50% of each day, and children must adjust to many caregivers on a daily or weekly basis, score "Yes."

1.4. "Frequent" means at least 75% of the time substitutes are used.

Questions

1.1, 3.1, 5.1. How many staff members work with this group every day? Who are the main staff members working with this group?

1.2, 3.2, 5.2. How are children assigned to groups? How often are children moved to another group?

1.3, 3.3, 5.3. How is the transition to a new group handled?

1.4, 3.4, 5.4, 7.3. How frequently are substitutes needed? Who are the substitutes for staff? How are they prepared to be substitutes?

7.2. May a child stay with the same staff or group for more than a year?

Inadequate		Minimal		Good		Excellent
1	2	3	4	5	6	7

38. Supervision and evaluation of staff*

1.1 No supervision provided for staff.*

1.2 No feedback or evaluation provided about staff performance.

3.1 Some supervision provided for staff (Ex. director observes informally; observation done in case of complaint).

3.2 Some feedback about performance provided.*

5.1 Annual supervisory observation provided.

5.2 Written evaluation of performance shared with staff at least yearly.

5.3 Strengths of staff as well as areas needing improvement identified in the evaluation.

5.4 Action is taken to implement the recommendation of the evaluation (Ex. training given to improve performance; new materials purchased, if needed).

7.1 Staff members participate in self-evaluation.*

7.2 Frequent observations and feedback given to staff in addition to annual observation.

7.3 Feedback from supervision is given in a helpful, supportive manner.

*Notes for Clarification

Item 38. Score this item NA only when the program is a 1-person operation with no other staff.

1.1. Get information to score this item by asking questions of the person being supervised, not the supervisor. In cases where classroom staff state that they do not know the answers to your questions, ask their supervisor.

3.2. Feedback may be verbal or in writing and may be fairly general at the minimal level of quality.

7.1. Give credit if staff participate in self-evaluation at least annually.

Questions

1.1, 3.1, 5.1, 5.2. Is your work supervised in any way? How is this done?

1.2, 3.2, 5.2, 7.3. Are you ever given any feedback about your performance? How is this handled? How often?

5.4. If improvement is needed, how is this handled?

7.1. Do you ever take part in self-evaluation? *If yes, ask:* How often?

Inadequate		Minimal		Good		Excellent
1	2	3	4	5	6	7

39. Opportunities for professional growth*

1.1 No orientation to program or in-service training provided for staff.

1.2 No staff meetings held.

3.1 Some orientation for new staff including emergency, safety, and health procedures given prior to working with children.*

3.2 Some in-service training provided.*

3.3 Some staff meetings held to handle administrative concerns.*

5.1 Thorough orientation for new staff including interaction with children and parents, discipline methods, appropriate activities.

5.2 Staff required to participate regularly in in-service training. (Ex. participate in community workshops; guest speakers and videos used for on-site training).*

5.3 Monthly staff meetings held that include staff development activities.

5.4 Some professional resource materials available on-site (Ex. books, magazines, or other materials on child development, cultural sensitivity, and classroom activities; resources may be borrowed from library).*

7.1 Support available for staff to attend courses, conferences, or workshops not provided by the program (Ex. released time, travel costs, conference fees).

7.2 Good professional library containing current materials on a variety of early childhood subjects available on premises.*

7.3 Staff members with less than an AA degree in early childhood education are required to continue formal education (Ex. work towards GED, CDA, AA).*
NA permitted.

(See Notes for Clarification and Questions on Next Page)

Item 39. Get information to score this item by asking questions of the classroom staff. If the staff members state that they do not know the answers to your questions, ask the supervisor.

3.1. Basic orientation must take place within 6 weeks after the start of employment including, at a minimum, emergency, health, and safety procedures, in order to give credit.

3.2. In-service training, which all classroom staff are required to attend, must be provided at least once a year in order to give credit.

3.3. Staff meetings, which all classroom staff are expected to attend, must be held at least 2 times a year by the director and/or administrative staff in order to get credit.

5.2. In-service training, which all classroom staff are required to attend, must be provided at least 2 times a year, either on-site or in community workshops.

5.4. "Some" means that at least 25 books, pamphlets, or AV materials in good condition are available to staff.

7.2. "Current materials" means that most of the books have been published within the last 10 years and journals and magazines are from the past 2 years. Books, such as the works of Piaget and Erikson, are exceptions, since they are classics on which many of our current ideas are based. At least 60 books and 3 series of periodicals that belong to the center are required to give credit.

7.3. AA/AS degree = Associate of Arts or Science (2-year degree)
CDA credential = Child Development Associate (1-year program)
GED = General Equivalency Degree (high school equivalency)

1.1, 3.1, 3.2, 5.1, 5.2. Is any training provided to staff? Please describe this training. What is done with new staff?

1.2, 3.3, 5.3. Do you have staff meetings? About how often? What is usually handled at these meetings?

5.4, 7.2. Are there any resources on-site that you can use for new ideas? *If yes, ask:* What is included? May I see them?

7.1. Is there any support provided so you can attend conferences or courses? Please describe what is available.

7.3. Are there any requirements for staff with less than an AA degree to continue their formal education? Please describe the requirements.

Sample of a Filled-in Score Sheet and Profile

Sample Score Sheet: Observation 1, 8/6/02

LISTENING AND TALKING

12. Helping children understand language   1 2 ③ 4 5 6 7

Y N	Y N	Y N	Y N
1.1 ☐ ☑	3.1 ☑ ☐	5.1 ☑ ☐	7.1 ☐ ☐
1.2 ☐ ☑	3.2 ☑ ☐	5.2 ☐ ☑	7.2 ☐ ☐
1.3 ☐ ☑	3.3 ☑ ☐	5.3 ☐ ☑	7.3 ☐ ☐
	3.4 ☑ ☐	5.4 ☐ ☑	

frequent social talk: "How's my little fellow?" "Such a cute girl." few names used, no labeling of objects

13. Helping children use language   1 2 ③ 4 5 6 7

Y N	Y N	Y N	Y N NA
1.1 ☐ ☑	3.1 ☑ ☐	5.1 ☐ ☑	7.1 ☐ ☐
1.2 ☐ ☑	3.2 ☑ ☐	5.2 ☐ ☑	7.2 ☐ ☐ ☐
		5.3 ☐ ☑	7.3 ☐ ☐
			7.4 ☐ ☐

long waiting before crying is answered about 30% of time. No verbal response.

14. Using books   1 2 3 4 ⑤ 6 7

Y N	Y N	Y N	Y N NA
1.1 ☐ ☑	3.1 ☑ ☐	5.1 ☑ ☐	7.1 ☐ ☐ ☑
1.2 ☐ ☑	3.2 ☑ ☐	5.2 ☑ ☐	7.2 ☐ ☑
1.3 ☐ ☑	3.3 ☑ ☐	5.3 ☑ ☐	7.3 ☐ ☑
	3.4 ☑ ☐	5.4 ☑ ☐	

17 books accessible. 1 teacher read informally to 3 interested children.

A. Subscale (Items 12 – 14) score 11

B. Number of items scored 3

LISTENING AND TALKING Average Score (A ÷ B) 3.67

Sample Score Sheet: Observation 2, 11/8/02

LISTENING AND TALKING

12. Helping children understand language   1 2 3 4 5 ⑥ 7

Y N	Y N	Y N	Y N
1.1 ☐ ☑	3.1 ☑ ☐	5.1 ☑ ☐	7.1 ☐ ☑
1.2 ☐ ☑	3.2 ☑ ☐	5.2 ☑ ☐	7.2 ☑ ☐
1.3 ☐ ☑	3.3 ☑ ☐	5.3 ☑ ☐	7.3 ☑ ☐
	3.4 ☑ ☐	5.4 ☑ ☐	

"Here's your cup, Sarah. You are holding it!" "Get the ball, Nathan. It's rolling." much talking like examples observed.

13. Helping children use language   1 2 3 4 ⑤ 6 7

Y N	Y N	Y N	Y N NA
1.1 ☐ ☑	3.1 ☑ ☐	5.1 ☑ ☐	7.1 ☐ ☑
1.2 ☐ ☑	3.2 ☑ ☐	5.2 ☑ ☐	7.2 ☐ ☑
		5.3 ☑ ☐	7.3 ☐ ☑
			7.4 ☐ ☑

Questions rare. Staff do most of talking. No notice of 1 child who uses 1 word sentences. regular timely responses.

14. Using books   1 2 3 4 ⑤ 6 7

Y N	Y N	Y N	Y N NA
1.1 ☐ ☑	3.1 ☑ ☐	5.1 ☑ ☐	7.1 ☐ ☑ ☐
1.2 ☐ ☑	3.2 ☑ ☐	5.2 ☑ ☐	7.2 ☑ ☐
1.3 ☐ ☑	3.3 ☑ ☐	5.3 ☑ ☐	7.3 ☐ ☑
	3.4 ☑ ☐	5.4 ☑ ☐	

no book area for children over 12 months. 7.3 teacher report

A. Subscale (Items 12 – 14) score 16

B. Number of items scored 3

LISTENING AND TALKING Average Score (A ÷ B) 5.33

Sample of a Profile

III. Listening and Talking (12-14)

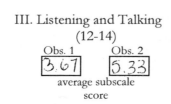

Obs. 1	Obs. 2
3.67	5.33

average subscale score

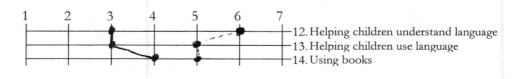

12. Helping children understand language
13. Helping children use language
14. Using books

SCORE SHEET–EXPANDED VERSION
Infant/Toddler Environment Rating Scale–Revised
Thelma Harms, Debby Cryer, and Richard M. Clifford

Observer: _____ Observer Code: ___ ___ ___

Center/School: _____ Center Code: ___ ___ ___

Room: _____ Room Code: ___ ___

Teacher(s): _____ Teacher Code: ___ ___

Number of staff present: ___ ___

Number of children enrolled in class: ___ ___

Highest number center allows in class at one time: ___ ___

Highest number of children present during observation: ___ ___

Date of Observation: ___ ___ / ___ ___ / ___ ___
m m d d y y

Number of children with identified disabilities: ___ ___

Check type(s) of disability: ☐ physical/sensory ☐ cognitive/language
☐ social/emotional ☐ other:_____

Birthdates of children enrolled: youngest ___ ___ / ___ ___ / ___ ___
m m d d y y
oldest ___ ___ / ___ ___ / ___ ___
m m d d y y

Time observation began: ___ ___ : ___ ___ ☐ AM ☐ PM

Time observation ended: ___ ___ : ___ ___ ☐ AM ☐ PM

Time interview began: ___ ___ : ___ ___ ☐ AM ☐ PM

Time interview ended: ___ ___ : ___ ___ ☐ AM ☐ PM

SPACE AND FURNISHINGS

1. Indoor space | 1 2 3 4 5 6 7 | 3.5, 5.3. Accessibility:

Y N	Y N NA	Y N	Y N
1.1 ☐ ☐	3.1 ☐ ☐	5.1 ☐ ☐	7.1 ☐ ☐
1.2 ☐ ☐	3.2 ☐ ☐	5.2 ☐ ☐	7.2 ☐ ☐
1.3 ☐ ☐	3.3 ☐ ☐	5.3 ☐ ☐	7.3 ☐ ☐
1.4 ☐ ☐	3.4 ☐ ☐		
	3.5 ☐ ☐ ☐		

2. Furniture for routine care and play | 1 2 3 4 5 6 7 | 5.2, 7.2. Child-sized table(s) and chairs?

Y N	Y N	Y N NA	Y N NA
1.1 ☐ ☐	3.1 ☐ ☐	5.1 ☐ ☐	7.1 ☐ ☐
1.2 ☐ ☐	3.2 ☐ ☐	5.2 ☐ ☐ ☐	7.2 ☐ ☐ ☐
1.3 ☐ ☐	3.3 ☐ ☐	5.3 ☐ ☐	7.3 ☐ ☐
	3.4 ☐ ☐	5.4 ☐ ☐	7.4 ☐ ☐
		5.5 ☐ ☐	

3. Provision for relaxation and comfort	1 2 3 4 5 6 7	3.1. Furnishings: 5.1. Cozy area? {y / n} 3.2, 5.3. Number of soft toys:

Y N   Y N   Y N   Y N NA
1.1 ☐ ☐   3.1 ☐ ☐   5.1 ☐ ☐   7.1 ☐ ☐
          3.2 ☐ ☐   5.2 ☐ ☐   7.2 ☐ ☐ ☐
                   5.3 ☐ ☐   7.3 ☐ ☐

4. Room arrangement	1 2 3 4 5 6 7	1.2, 3.2, 5.2. Problems with visual supervision

Y N   Y N NA   Y N   Y N
1.1 ☐ ☐   3.1 ☐ ☐   5.1 ☐ ☐   7.1 ☐ ☐
1.2 ☐ ☐   3.2 ☐ ☐   5.2 ☐ ☐   7.2 ☐ ☐
          3.3 ☐ ☐ ☐   5.3 ☐ ☐   7.3 ☐ ☐
                       5.4 ☐ ☐

5. Display for children	1 2 3 4 5 6 7	5.4. Staff talk about display? (Observe 1 example)

Y N   Y N   Y N   Y N NA
1.1 ☐ ☐   3.1 ☐ ☐   5.1 ☐ ☐   7.1 ☐ ☐
1.2 ☐ ☐   3.2 ☐ ☐   5.2 ☐ ☐   7.2 ☐ ☐
                   5.3 ☐ ☐   7.3 ☐ ☐
                   5.4 ☐ ☐   7.4 ☐ ☐ ☐

A. Subscale (Items 1–5) Score __ __   B. Number of items scored __ __   **SPACE AND FURNISHINGS Average Score (A ÷ B)** __.__ __

PERSONAL CARE ROUTINES

6. Greeting/departing	1 2 3 4 5 6 7	1.1, 3.1, 3.4, 5.1, 7.2. Greetings observed (√ = yes, X = no, W = warm)

                                Child   Parent   Info. shared

Y N   Y N   Y N NA   Y N NA
1.1 ☐ ☐   3.1 ☐ ☐   5.1 ☐ ☐   7.1 ☐ ☐
1.2 ☐ ☐   3.2 ☐ ☐   5.2 ☐ ☐   7.2 ☐ ☐
1.3 ☐ ☐   3.3 ☐ ☐   5.3 ☐ ☐ ☐   7.3 ☐ ☐ ☐
          3.4 ☐ ☐

1. ____ ____ ____
2. ____ ____ ____
3. ____ ____ ____
4. ____ ____ ____
5. ____ ____ ____
6. ____ ____ ____
7. ____ ____ ____
8. ____ ____ ____

7. Meals/snacks

1	2	3	4	5	6	7

	Y	N	NA		Y	N	NA		Y	N	NA		Y	N
1.1	☐	☐		3.1	☐	☐		5.1	☐	☐		7.1	☐	☐
1.2	☐	☐		3.2	☐	☐		5.2	☐	☐		7.2	☐	☐
1.3	☐	☐		3.3	☐	☐		5.3	☐	☐				
1.4	☐	☐		3.4	☐	☐		5.4	☐	☐				
1.5	☐	☐	☐	3.5	☐	☐	☐	5.5	☐	☐	☐			

1.3, 3.3, 5.3. Handwashing: (√ = yes, X = no)

	Children		Adults	
Before eating		Before food prep, feeding	
After eating		After feeding	

1.3, 3.3, 5.3. Same sink used? {y / n}

Sink sanitized? {y / n}

Tables/highchair tray washed, sanitized? {y / n}

8. Nap

1	2	3	4	5	6	7	NA

	Y	N		Y	N		Y	N	NA		Y	N
1.1	☐	☐	3.1	☐	☐	5.1	☐	☐		7.1	☐	☐
1.2	☐	☐	3.2	☐	☐	5.2	☐	☐	☐	7.2	☐	☐
1.3	☐	☐	3.3	☐	☐	5.3	☐	☐				
			3.4	☐	☐							

1.1. All cots/ mats, cribs > 36" apart or solid barrier? {y / n}

Other issues:

9. Diapering/toileting

1	2	3	4	5	6	7

	Y	N		Y	N		Y	N		Y	N	NA
1.1	☐	☐	3.1	☐	☐	5.1	☐	☐	7.1	☐	☐	
1.2	☐	☐	3.2	☐	☐	5.2	☐	☐	7.2	☐	☐	☐
1.3	☐	☐	3.3	☐	☐	5.3	☐	☐	7.3	☐	☐	
1.4	☐	☐	3.4	☐	☐	5.4	☐	☐				

1.1, 3.1. Diapering procedure (every adult observed): (√ = yes, X = no)

Prep								
Proper disposal								
Wipe child's hands								
Wipe adult's hands								
Sanitize diaper area								
Same sink sanitized								

Other issues:

1.1, 3.1. Same sink sanitized? {y / n}

1.3, 3.3. Handwashing

Adult							
Child							

10. Health practices

1	2	3	4	5	6	7

	Y	N		Y	N	NA		Y	N	NA		Y	N	NA
1.1	☐	☐	3.1	☐	☐		5.1	☐	☐		7.1	☐	☐	
1.2	☐	☐	3.2	☐	☐		5.2	☐	☐		7.2	☐	☐	☐
1.3	☐	☐	3.3	☐	☐		5.3	☐	☐		7.3	☐	☐	
			3.4	☐	☐	☐	5.4	☐	☐	☐				

1.1, 3.2, 5.2. Handwashing observations: (√ = yes, X = no)

	Child	Adult
Upon arrival in class or re-entry from outside		
Before water; after sand, water, messy play		
After dealing with bodily fluids		
After touching pets or contaminated objects		

11. Safety practices

1	2	3	4	5	6	7

	Y	N		Y	N		Y	N		Y	N
1.1	☐	☐	3.1	☐	☐	5.1	☐	☐	7.1	☐	☐
1.2	☐	☐	3.2	☐	☐	5.2	☐	☐	7.2	☐	☐
1.3	☐	☐	3.3	☐	☐						

1.1, 1.2, 3.1, 5.1. Safety hazards:

	Major	Minor
Indoor:		
Outdoor:		

A. Subscale (Items 6–11) Score __ __   B. Number of items scored __ __   **PERSONAL CARE ROUTINES Average Score (A ÷ B)** __.__ __

LISTENING AND TALKING

12. Helping children understand language

| 1 | 2 | 3 | 4 | 5 | 6 | 7 |

	Y	N			Y	N			Y	N			Y	N
1.1	☐	☐	3.1	☐	☐	5.1	☐	☐	7.1	☐	☐
1.2	☐	☐	3.2	☐	☐	5.2	☐	☐	7.2	☐	☐
1.3	☐	☐	3.3	☐	☐	5.3	☐	☐	7.3	☐	☐
			3.4	☐	☐	5.4	☐	☐			

3.1, 5.1. During routines:

During play:

5.4, 7.1. Examples of descriptive words used:

7.2. Examples of observed verbal play:

13. Helping children use language

| 1 | 2 | 3 | 4 | 5 | 6 | 7 |

	Y	N			Y	N			Y	N			Y	N	NA
1.1	☐	☐	3.1	☐	☐	5.1	☐	☐	7.1	☐	☐	
1.2	☐	☐	3.2	☐	☐	5.2	☐	☐	7.2	☐	☐	☐
						5.3	☐	☐	7.3	☐	☐	
									7.4	☐	☐	

7.2. Staff add words/ideas to what children say (observe 2 examples):

7.3. Staff ask simple questions (observe 2 examples):

14. Using books

| 1 | 2 | 3 | 4 | 5 | 6 | 7 |

	Y	N			Y	N			Y	N			Y	N	NA
1.1	☐	☐	3.1	☐	☐	5.1	☐	☐	7.1	☐	☐	☐
1.2	☐	☐	3.2	☐	☐	5.2	☐	☐	7.2	☐	☐	
1.3	☐	☐	3.3	☐	☐	5.3	☐	☐	7.3	☐	☐	
			3.4	☐	☐	5.4	☐	☐				

1.2, 3.2. Number of books in disrepair:

5.1. Any inappropriate books: {y / n}
(violent, frightening)

5.3. Staff read to individuals/small groups: {y / n}
(observed at least 1 example)

5.2. Wide selection of books
Races: _____
Ages: _____
Abilities: _____
Animals : _____
Familiar routines: _____
Familiar objects: _____

Nature science books for Item 22:

A. Subscale (Items 12–14) Score __ __   B. Number of items scored __ __   **LISTENING AND TALKING Average Score (A ÷ B)** __.__ __

ACTIVITIES

15. Fine motor

| 1 2 3 4 5 6 7 |

	Y N		Y N		Y N		Y N
1.1	□ □	3.1	□ □	5.1	□ □	7.1	□ □
1.2	□ □	3.2	□ □	5.2	□ □	7.2	□ □
		3.3	□ □				

1.1, 3.1, 5.1.
Materials for infants:

Materials for toddlers:

16. Active physical play

| 1 2 3 4 5 6 7 |

	Y N		Y N		Y N		Y N
1.1	□ □	3.1	□ □	5.1	□ □	7.1	□ □
1.2	□ □	3.2	□ □	5.2	□ □	7.2	□ □
1.3	□ □	3.3	□ □	5.3	□ □	7.3	□ □
				5.4	□ □		
				5.5	□ □		

1.1, 1.2, 3.3, 5.5.
Any equipment/materials inappropriate/unsafe?

Appropriate indoor/outdoor space:

17. Art

| 1 2 3 4 5 6 7 NA |

	Y N		Y N NA		Y N NA		Y N
1.1	□ □	3.1	□ □ □	5.1	□ □ □	7.1	□ □
1.2	□ □	3.2	□ □	5.2	□ □	7.2	□ □
		3.3	□ □	5.3	□ □		

1.2. Toxic/unsafe art materials used? {y / n}

3.2. Appropriate/safe/nontoxic art materials used

18. Music and movement

| 1 2 3 4 5 6 7 |

	Y N		Y N		Y N		Y N
1.1	□ □	3.1	□ □	5.1	□ □	7.1	□ □
1.2	□ □	3.2	□ □	5.2	□ □	7.2	□ □
		3.3	□ □	5.3	□ □	7.3	□ □
				5.4	□ □		

3.1, 5.1. List number of musical toys/instruments:

5.2. Informal singing observed? {y / n}

19. Blocks

| 1 2 3 4 5 6 7 NA |

	Y N		Y N		Y N		Y N
1.1	□ □	3.1	□ □	5.1	□ □	7.1	□ □
		3.2	□ □	5.2	□ □	7.2	□ □
		3.3	□ □	5.3	□ □	7.3	□ □

3.1, 5.1, 7.1. Sets of blocks:
1)

2)

3)

3.2, 7.2. Accessories:

20. Dramatic play

| 1 2 3 4 5 6 7 |

		Y N	Y N NA	Y N NA
	Y N	Y N		
1.1 ☐ ☐	3.1 ☐ ☐	5.1 ☐ ☐	7.1 ☐ ☐	
	3.2 ☐ ☐	5.2 ☐ ☐	7.2 ☐ ☐ ☐	
		5.3 ☐ ☐	7.3 ☐ ☐	
		5.4 ☐ ☐ ☐		

5.1 Dramatic play materials:

Infants **and** toddlers:
Dolls–
Soft animals–
Toy telephones–
Pots & pans–

Toddlers **only**:
Dress-ups–
Child-sized play furniture–
Play foods–
Dishes/eating utensils–
Doll furniture–
Small play buildings & accessories–

21. Sand and water play

| 1 2 3 4 5 6 7 NA |

Y N	Y N	Y N	Y N
1.1 ☐ ☐	3.1 ☐ ☐	5.1 ☐ ☐	7.1 ☐ ☐
	3.2 ☐ ☐	5.2 ☐ ☐	7.2 ☐ ☐
	3.3 ☐ ☐	5.3 ☐ ☐	

22. Nature/science

| 1 2 3 4 5 6 7 |

Y N	Y N	Y N	Y N
1.1 ☐ ☐	3.1 ☐ ☐	5.1 ☐ ☐	7.1 ☐ ☐
1.2 ☐ ☐	3.2 ☐ ☐	5.2 ☐ ☐	7.2 ☐ ☐
	3.3 ☐ ☐	5.3 ☐ ☐	

5.3. Example of science/nature observed in daily events:

23. Use of TV, video, and/or computer

| 1 2 3 4 5 6 7 NA |

Y N NA	Y N	Y N	Y N
1.1 ☐ ☐	3.1 ☐ ☐	5.1 ☐ ☐	7.1 ☐ ☐
1.2 ☐ ☐	3.2 ☐ ☐	5.2 ☐ ☐	7.2 ☐ ☐
1.3 ☐ ☐ ☐	3.3 ☐ ☐	5.3 ☐ ☐	

24. Promoting acceptance of diversity

| 1 2 3 4 5 6 7 |

Y N	Y N	Y N	Y N
1.1 ☐ ☐	3.1 ☐ ☐	5.1 ☐ ☐	7.1 ☐ ☐
1.2 ☐ ☐	3.2 ☐ ☐	5.2 ☐ ☐	7.2 ☐ ☐
1.3 ☐ ☐	3.3 ☐ ☐		

5.1. Diversity in materials (10 examples, all types of categories):

	Books	Pictures	Materials
Races/Cultures			
Ages			
Abilities			
Gender			

5.2. Dolls (3 different skin tones/facial features):

7.1. Non-sexist images:

7.2. Variety of activities:

A. Subscale (Items 15–24) Score __ __   B. Number of items scored __ __   **ACTIVITIES Average Score (A ÷ B)** __.__ __

INTERACTION

25. Supervision of play and learning | 1 2 3 4 5 6 7

Y N	Y N	Y N	Y N
1.1 ☐ ☐	3.1 ☐ ☐	5.1 ☐ ☐	7.1 ☐ ☐
	3.2 ☐ ☐	5.2 ☐ ☐	7.2 ☐ ☐
		5.3 ☐ ☐	7.3 ☐ ☐
		5.4 ☐ ☐	

26. Peer interaction | 1 2 3 4 5 6 7

Y N	Y N	Y N	Y N
1.1 ☐ ☐	3.1 ☐ ☐	5.1 ☐ ☐	7.1 ☐ ☐
1.2 ☐ ☐	3.2 ☐ ☐	5.2 ☐ ☐	7.2 ☐ ☐

7.1. Staff explain actions/intensions/feelings (observe 2 examples):

7.2. Positive social interaction talked about (observe 1 example):

27. Staff-child interaction | 1 2 3 4 5 6 7

Y N	Y N	Y N	Y N
1.1 ☐ ☐	3.1 ☐ ☐	5.1 ☐ ☐	7.1 ☐ ☐
1.2 ☐ ☐	3.2 ☐ ☐	5.2 ☐ ☐	7.2 ☐ ☐
1.3 ☐ ☐	3.3 ☐ ☐	5.3 ☐ ☐	
	3.4 ☐ ☐		

28. Discipline | 1 2 3 4 5 6 7

Y N	Y N	Y N	Y N
1.1 ☐ ☐	3.1 ☐ ☐	5.1 ☐ ☐	7.1 ☐ ☐
1.2 ☐ ☐	3.2 ☐ ☐	5.2 ☐ ☐	7.2 ☐ ☐
	3.3 ☐ ☐	5.3 ☐ ☐	7.3 ☐ ☐
		5.4 ☐ ☐	

A. Subscale (Items 25–28) Score __ __   B. Number of items scored __ __   **INTERACTION** Average Score (A ÷ B) __.__ __

PROGRAM STRUCTURE

29. Schedule

| 1 | 2 | 3 | 4 | 5 | 6 | 7 |

5.4. Example of more than 3-minute wait, or obvious distress while waiting:

	Y N		Y N		Y N		Y N
1.1	☐ ☐	3.1	☐ ☐	5.1	☐ ☐	7.1	☐ ☐
1.2	☐ ☐	3.2	☐ ☐	5.2	☐ ☐	7.2	☐ ☐
1.3	☐ ☐			5.3	☐ ☐		
				5.4	☐ ☐		

30. Free play

| 1 | 2 | 3 | 4 | 5 | 6 | 7 |

7.1. Supervision as educational interaction (observe 2 examples):

	Y N		Y N		Y N		Y N
1.1	☐ ☐	3.1	☐ ☐	5.1	☐ ☐	7.1	☐ ☐
1.2	☐ ☐	3.2	☐ ☐	5.2	☐ ☐	7.2	☐ ☐
		3.3	☐ ☐	5.3	☐ ☐		

31. Group play activities

| 1 | 2 | 3 | 4 | 5 | 6 | 7 | NA |

	Y N		Y N		Y N		Y N
1.1	☐ ☐	3.1	☐ ☐	5.1	☐ ☐	7.1	☐ ☐
1.2	☐ ☐	3.2	☐ ☐	5.2	☐ ☐	7.2	☐ ☐
1.3	☐ ☐	3.3	☐ ☐	5.3	☐ ☐		

32. Provisions for children with disabilities

| 1 | 2 | 3 | 4 | 5 | 6 | 7 | NA |

	Y N		Y N		Y N		Y N
1.1	☐ ☐	3.1	☐ ☐	5.1	☐ ☐	7.1	☐ ☐
1.2	☐ ☐	3.2	☐ ☐	5.2	☐ ☐	7.2	☐ ☐
1.3	☐ ☐	3.3	☐ ☐	5.3	☐ ☐	7.3	☐ ☐
1.4	☐ ☐	3.4	☐ ☐				

A. Subscale (Items 29–32) Score __ __   B. Number of items scored __ __   **PROGRAM STRUCTURE Average Score (A ÷ B)** __.__ __

PARENTS AND STAFF

33. Provisions for parents

| 1 | 2 | 3 | 4 | 5 | 6 | 7 |

	Y N		Y N		Y N		Y N
1.1	☐ ☐	3.1	☐ ☐	5.1	☐ ☐	7.1	☐ ☐
1.2	☐ ☐	3.2	☐ ☐	5.2	☐ ☐	7.2	☐ ☐
		3.3	☐ ☐	5.3	☐ ☐	7.3	☐ ☐
		3.4	☐ ☐	5.4	☐ ☐		

34. Provisions for personal needs of staff

| 1 | 2 | 3 | 4 | 5 | 6 | 7 |

	Y N		Y N NA		Y N		Y N
1.1	☐ ☐	3.1	☐ ☐	5.1	☐ ☐	7.1	☐ ☐
1.2	☐ ☐	3.2	☐ ☐	5.2	☐ ☐	7.2	☐ ☐
		3.3	☐ ☐	5.3	☐ ☐	7.3	☐ ☐
		3.4	☐ ☐	5.4	☐ ☐		
		3.5	☐ ☐ ☐	5.5	☐ ☐		

35. Provisions for professional needs of staff

| 1 | 2 | 3 | 4 | 5 | 6 | 7 |

	Y N		Y N		Y N		Y N
1.1	☐ ☐	3.1	☐ ☐	5.1	☐ ☐	7.1	☐ ☐
1.2	☐ ☐	3.2	☐ ☐	5.2	☐ ☐	7.2	☐ ☐
1.3	☐ ☐	3.3	☐ ☐	5.3	☐ ☐		

36. Staff interaction and cooperation

| 1 | 2 | 3 | 4 | 5 | 6 | 7 | NA |

	Y N		Y N		Y N		Y N
1.1	☐ ☐	3.1	☐ ☐	5.1	☐ ☐	7.1	☐ ☐
1.2	☐ ☐	3.2	☐ ☐	5.2	☐ ☐	7.2	☐ ☐
1.3	☐ ☐	3.3	☐ ☐	5.3	☐ ☐	7.3	☐ ☐

37. Staff continuity

| 1 | 2 | 3 | 4 | 5 | 6 | 7 |

	Y N		Y N		Y N		Y N
1.1	☐ ☐	3.1	☐ ☐	5.1	☐ ☐	7.1	☐ ☐
1.2	☐ ☐	3.2	☐ ☐	5.2	☐ ☐	7.2	☐ ☐
1.3	☐ ☐	3.3	☐ ☐	5.3	☐ ☐	7.3	☐ ☐
1.4	☐ ☐	3.4	☐ ☐	5.4	☐ ☐		

38. Supervision and evaluation of staff

| 1 2 3 4 5 6 7 NA |

	Y N		Y N		Y N		Y N
1.1	☐ ☐	3.1	☐ ☐	5.1	☐ ☐	7.1	☐ ☐
1.2	☐ ☐	3.2	☐ ☐	5.2	☐ ☐	7.2	☐ ☐
				5.3	☐ ☐	7.3	☐ ☐
				5.4	☐ ☐		

39. Opportunities for professional growth

| 1 2 3 4 5 6 7 |

	Y N		Y N		Y N		Y N NA
1.1	☐ ☐	3.1	☐ ☐	5.1	☐ ☐	7.1	☐ ☐
1.2	☐ ☐	3.2	☐ ☐	5.2	☐ ☐	7.2	☐ ☐
		3.3	☐ ☐	5.3	☐ ☐	7.3	☐ ☐ ☐
				5.4	☐ ☐		

A. Subscale (Items 33–39) Score __ __   B. Number of items scored __ __   **PARENTS AND STAFF Average Score (A ÷ B)** __.__ __

Total and Average Score

	Subscale/Total Score		# of Items Scored		Average Score
Space and Furnishings	_____	÷	_____	=	_____
Personal Care Routines	_____	÷	_____	=	_____
Listening and Talking	_____	÷	_____	=	_____
Activities	_____	÷	_____	=	_____
Interaction	_____	÷	_____	=	_____
Program Structure	_____	÷	_____	=	_____
Parents and Staff	_____	÷	_____	=	_____
TOTAL	_____	÷	_____	=	_____

ITERS-R Profile

Center/School: _____

Teacher(s)/Classroom: _____

Observation 1: ___/___ ___/___ ___/___
            m m d d y y

Observation 2: ___/___ ___/___ ___/___
            m m d d y y

Observer: _____

Observer: _____

Scale: 1 2 3 4 5 6 7

I. Space and Furnishings (1–5)
1. Indoor space
2. Furniture for routine care and play
3. Provision for relaxation and comfort
4. Room arrangement
5. Display for children

Obs. 1 ☐   Obs. 2 ☐   average subscale score ☐

II. Personal Care Routines (6–11)
6. Greeting/departing
7. Meals/snacks
8. Nap
9. Diapering/toileting
10. Health practices
11. Safety practices

☐   ☐

III. Listening and Talking (12–14)
12. Helping children understand language
13. Helping children use language
14. Using books

☐   ☐

IV. Activities (15–24)
15. Fine motor
16. Active physical play
17. Art
18. Music and movement
19. Blocks
20. Dramatic play
21. Sand and water play
22. Nature/science
23. Use of TV, video, and/or computers
24. Promoting acceptance of diversity

☐   ☐

V. Interaction (25–28)
25. Supervision of play and learning
26. Peer interaction
27. Staff–child interaction
28. Discipline

☐   ☐

VI. Program Structure (29–32)
29. Schedule
30. Free play
31. Group play activities
32. Provisions for children with disabilities

☐   ☐

VII. Parents and Staff (33–39)
33. Provisions for parents
34. Provisions for personal needs of staff
35. Provisions for professional needs of staff
36. Staff interaction and cooperation
37. Staff continuity
38. Supervision and evaluation of staff
39. Opportunities for professional growth

☐   ☐

Average Subscale Scores

SPACE AND FURNISHING
PERSONAL CARE ROUTINES
LISTENING AND TALKING
ACTIVITIES
INTERACTION
PROGRAM STRUCTURE
PARENTS AND STAFF

1 2 3 4 5 6 7